Coding for Kids in Python

Contents

Disclaimer

Copyright © 2020

All Rights Reserved

No part of this eBook can be transmitted or reproduced in any form including print, electronic, photocopying, scanning, mechanical or recording without prior written permission from the author. While the author has taken utmost efforts to ensure the accuracy of the written content, all readers are advised to follow information mentioned herein at their own risk. The author cannot be held responsible for any personal or commercial damage caused by information. All readers are encouraged to seek professional advice when needed.

Introduction

In the 21 century there is nothing around us that works without computers. Computers are everywhere around us. Mobile phones, laptops, ATMs, you name it. They have computers inside them. In addition, there are other machines with embedded computers hidden inside them. These include items like washing machines, dryers, refrigerators, car, vehicles, air conditioners and elevators, which have some sort of computer chip inside them. How do we tell computers how to work? It is through programming!

A programming language is a language that a machine can understand and run to perform various tasks. It is how we communicate with machines to make them understand what we want to accomplish.

A program is a logical sequential statement that perform a task. A program can be in any programming language we want. It can even be in 1s and 0s which is only thing that a computer understands. Everything in a computer is in 1s and 0s. A high level programing language uses English like language so we can program computers easily. Ultimately, any program in any language is converted into 1s and 0s so that a machine can understand.

Technology is already everywhere in our daily lives and it is increasing at an unprecedented rate. All this technology needs to be invented, programed and maintained! It is only through understanding computers that we can do all of this and maintain and develop technologies to get further ahead.

There are hundreds of programming language around. Though many languages are no longer used, some remain very popular and used widely like Java, JavaScript, C#, C++, PHP, Python, Swift, SQL, Ruby.

No one knows all these languages and actually no one can learn all of them because they are so vast and many. The good news is that you don't need to learn them all. One good popular language suffices. You can get started and code what you need using only one language. Once you start picking things up and learn enough, any other language will be easy and should take less time. The main concepts and fundamentals are similar in different programming languages.

In this book we will use the Python programming language. Python is a great and easy language to learn for beginners. There are so many libraries and ecosystems specific to Python.

This book focuses on learning by practice and experimentation. Programs and outputs are provided. You are advised to implement the actual program and compare it with the code in the book. After the program runs, you are encouraged to adapt the code for your own purpose.

There are exercises at the end of each chapter that help to solidify the learning of each concept and move forward. This is the best way to get the most out of this book.

Why Python is Great for Beginners

Python is a great programming language to learn. It's easy to learn and it is a good entry point into the world of programming. Python was invented by a person named Guido van Rossum, he was working on an educational project to build a language for new coders called ABC. As a result of this project he created the Python programming language. Guido made Python with four main goals in mind. These goals are to be intuitive, open source, easy to understand and to be versatile to allow for shorter development time. Python continues developing and maturing till today. Many enthusiasts and developers use it every day for a variety of tasks. Python is used for many tasks like web development, scripting, web scraping, data analysis and automation.

Here's why Python is great:

Shallow learning curve

Python takes little time to learn. This makes it a great language for beginners to start learning programing.

That is why it used in many introductory computer science courses around the world.

Intuitive

The syntax of Python is very easy to read. In fact, it reads very similar to English and that is one reason for its intuitiveness. The language is consistent overall and is easy to read. You don't have to spend time understanding arcane symbols and syntax. Code is read much more often than it is written. That's why readability is a great advantage for language to have.

Very little boilerplate

The "Hello World" program is a common basic program that is just one line of code. Simple programs like that can be written with very little "starting code" or additional codes. Python comes with powerful data types already built-in. Python has Lists, Dicts, Tuples, Sets, strings. These datatypes make it easy to start developing right away without having to implement those data structures from scratch. These data types (and many more) facilitate short development times and more flexible timelines.

Great Ecosystem

A programming language is of little value only by itself. What makes a programming language widely adopted and useful is the supporting community and libraries it has. There are lots of third-party libraries and people to help you.

Interpreted language

Python is a high-level scripting language (like PHP, Ruby, Perl, JavaScript, etc.). High level Languages of this type generally don't require variables to be declared in advance. They allow variables types to change. This called dynamic typing. Python in an interpretive language meaning programs can run directly without having to be compiled before execution.

Versatility

Python has many applications, including data science, machine learning, web development, and game development.

Here are some examples of Python modules.

- Pandas is used for data wrangling and analysis.
- matplotlib, a plotting library useful for plotting graphs using many sorts of graphs.
- Pygame for developing games
- Django, a framework for web development

Python emphasize fundamentals, the core philosophy of the language is "The Zen of Python". You can get them by typing on python "import this". The Zen of Python are:

1. Beautiful is better than ugly.
2. Explicit is better than implicit.
3. Simple is better than complex.
4. Complex is better than complicated.
5. Flat is better than nested.
6. Sparse is better than dense.
7. Readability counts.

Setting up python workspace

There are many ways to have a python environment to begin coding. I will illustrate here 2 easy methods to set up a python workspace.

Method 1 – Anaconda

Anaconda is an environment that comes with python and many other preinstalled libraries. You get them all as on package that is installed once. Anaconda come with a tool named Jupyter Lab, Jupyter lab is a great way to run python interactively. It is also used extensively in data science and python learning because of its ease of use.

This book uses mainly jupyter lab to run python scripts interactively.

To install Anaconda, follow the guideline below.

    1- Open up the link

https://www.anaconda.com/products/individual

Individual Edition

Your data science toolkit

With over 20 million users worldwide, the open-source Individual Edition (Distribution) is the easiest way to perform Python/R data science and machine learning on a single machine. Developed for solo practitioners, it is the toolkit that equips you to work with thousands of open-source packages and libraries.

Click the download **button an**d choose the version that correspond to your system

After downloading follow the instructions of installer to install it.

After installation locate "Anaconda Prompt (anaconda3)" on your system.

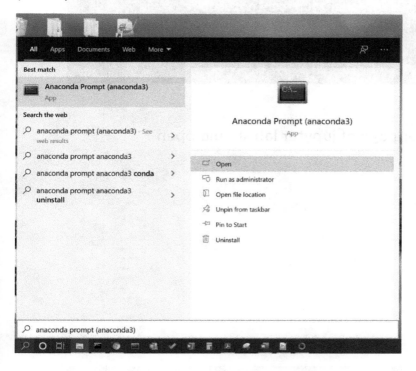

Click on "**Anaconda Prompt (anaconda3)**" to open it.

In the command prompt type "**jupyter notebook**" and press enter.

![Anaconda Prompt icon] Anaconda Prompt (anaconda3)

```
(base) C:\Users\omar>jupyter notebook
```

A browser page of jupyter lab should open

On the new box located on the top right corner click python 3.

Now you are ready to run python programs interactively.

To write a program type **"print("hello world")"** and click run or use shortcut shift + enter.

Congratulatons now you have your first program running .

Alternatively, If you prefer working on the cloud, you can run jupyter lab online using jupyter website.

Open https://jupyter.org/try

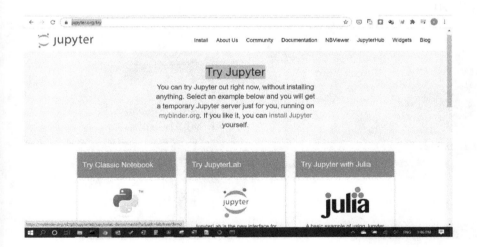

Click on **Try Jupyter lab**

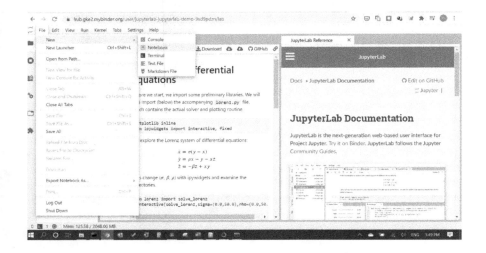

A page similar to the picture above should open, click on **File>New>Notebook**.

A prompt box will ask you about a kernel to choose, choose Python 3.

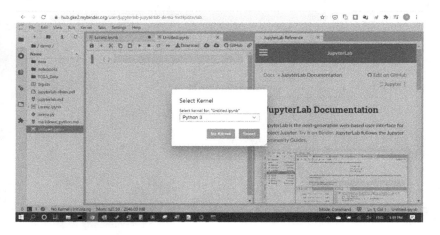

To write a program type **print("hello world")** and click run or use shortcut shift + enter.

Congratulatons now you have your first program running .

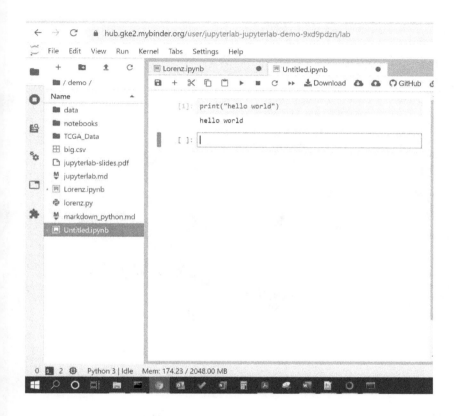

Method 2 – Installing python and a text editor

If you have large python programs it might be best to edit them using a text editor and the run them separately using python.

Step 1: install python

Open link https://www.python.org/downloads/ and download python.

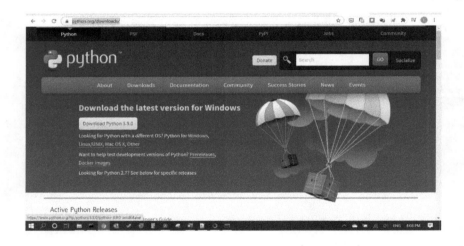

Open the installer package and install python .

Step 2: install Notepad ++

Notepad++ is an easy to use text editor for writing and editing codes .

Open URL: https://notepad-plus-plus.org/downloads/v7.9.1/

Download and install notepad++

Locate notepad++ on your system and open

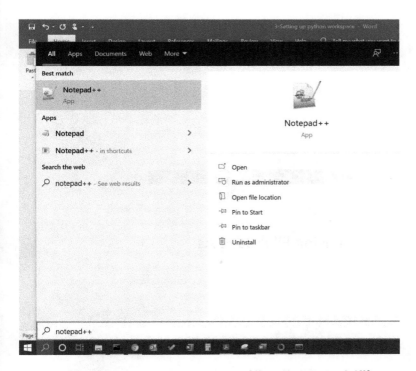

Write your first program **print("Hello, World")**

Save your program using File>Save As..

Name your program and save type as Python file

To run your program locate command Prompt on your system and open it.

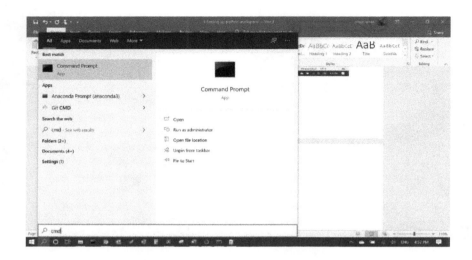

Access the folder where your python file resides by typing

cd "folder address" if your file is desktop then

type cd C:\Users\USER_NAME\Desktop

USER_NAME is specific to your user name on your Desktop and varies from computer to computer

```
Command Prompt
Microsoft Windows [Version 10.0.19041.630]
(c) 2020 Microsoft Corporation. All rights reserved.

C:\Users\omar>cd C:\Users\omar\Desktop\t
```

To run the program type

```
Command Prompt

C:\Users\omar\Desktop\t>python "new 1.py"
Hello World!

C:\Users\omar\Desktop\t>_
```

python "program_name", for example if program name is run.py

then type **python "run.py"**

Congratulation now you have you first program working.

Variables

Introduction to variables

Think of a variable as a container used to hold some value. A variable is a location in memory holding some value. In static type programming language such as c and c++ variable type must be declared beforehand and variable type cannot change anytime later. That is why we first declare the variable where we assign the value type then we assign a value to the variable.

Below is an example of variable declaration and assignment in a statically typed language.

int var;   Variable declaration of type integer.

var = 8;   Variable assignment to 8.

But since python is dynamically typed you don't have to declare variable type first, it will automatically work out the variable type for you. To define a variable, assign a value to variable name using equality sign. This is called assignment operator. The code below assigns three variables to a string, integer and a float.

```
1  # variables
2
3  lang = "python"
4  num1 = 2
5  num2 = 3.4
6
7  print(lang)
8  print(num1)
9  print(num2)
10 print('\n')
11
12 print(type(lang))
13 print(type(num1))
14 print(type(num2))
```

Output:

```
python
2
3.4


<class 'str'>
<class 'int'>
<class 'float'>
```

Observe that each variable has a type without being explicitly defined.

String variables are declared with either single quotes or double quotes.

we can define several variables on one line such as var1, var2, var3 = 1, 2, 3.

```
1  x, y, z = 1, 2, 3
2  print(x, y, z)
```

Output:

1 2 3

Variable Name Rules

In python variable names have few rules. The rules are

1. Variable name must start with a letter or "_" underscore.
2. Name of variables must be alphanumeric; no special characters are allowed.
3. Variable name is case sensitive A and a are different variables.

Example of different variable names.

```
1  num = 1
2  NUM = 2
3  _2num = 3
4  num2 = 4
5  num2_ = 5
6
7  print(num, NUM, _2num, num2, num2_)
```
1 2 3 4 5

Note that on the above snippet variables names were assigned a meaningful named. This is very important on programming as it makes reading programs easy to read.

Global and local Variables

Variables that are created outside functions are accessible to any function. They are called global functions. Global variables can be accessed by any function. Local variables are variables that are defined inside functions and cannot be accesses from outside function scopes.

In the code below "lang" variable is global so func() function can access it. When func() is called the output is python.

```
1  # this variable is global to this scope
2  lang = "Python"
3
4  def func():
5      print(lang)
6
7  func()
```
Python

```
1   # this variable is global to this scope
2   lang = "Python"
3
4   def func():
5       # this variable is local to this function
6       lang = "C++"
7       print(lang)
8
9   func()
10  print(lang)
```

C++
Python

Similarly, here "lang" variable is global, but we also have variable named lang that is equal to C++.When func() is called the output is C++ because the local variable inside func have precedence over global variable outside func. However, when we print variable lang we see that the global variable didn't change. That is because even though we have lang variable inside func and outside, there scopes are separate and they do not interfere/override with each other.

Assignment Operators

Assignments operators are used to assign values in python. They are also used to manipulate and update variable values. The table below shows assignment operators and their names. These operators are used as shorthand to their equivalents.

```
 1  a, b, c, d, e, f = 1, 1, 1, 1, 1, 1
 2
 3  a += 2
 4
 5  b -= 2
 6
 7  c *= 2
 8
 9  d /= 2
10
11  e %= 2
12
13  f **= 2
14
15  print("a is ", a)
16  print("b is ", b)
17  print("c is ", c)
18  print("d is ", d)
19  print("e is ", e)
20  print("f is ", f)

a is  3
b is  -1
c is  2
d is  0.5
e is  1
f is  1
```

Operator	Name	Example	Equivalent
=	Assignment operator	j = 2	j = 2
+=	Addition assignment	j += 2	j = j + 2
-=	Subtraction assignment	j -= 2	j = j - 2
*=	Multiplication assignment	j *= 2	j = j * 2
/=	Division assignment	j /= 2	j = j / 2
%=	Modulus assignment	j %= 2	j = j % 2
**=	Exponential assignment	j **= 2	j = j**2

The script below, assign all variables a, b, c, d, e, f in line 1, to 1. Then it uses assignment operator to update variables values. Investigate the output to understand how operator assignment work.

String methods

One of the most powerful aspects of python, is that it provides powerful functions right out of the box without having to re-implement them. String methods in python are versatile and so powerful that it spares you the need to spend time implementing them from scratch. You can easily manipulate string with them. In this section we will learn some of python string methods.

Here is list of common python string methods.

String concatenation: to concatenate two strings together just use + operator.

A = "Hello"

B = "World"

A + B _returns_ "Hello World"

Also multiplying a string by any number n repeats the string n times.

A = 5 * "hi"

A _returns_ "hihihihihi"

len(str) – length function returns string characters length.

len("python is amazing") - returns 17. Note that len count spaces too!

str[index] – indexing operator, selects a single character from string. The number inside the brackets is called index, it is an integer value. Indexing in python starts at zero.

a = "Python"

a[0] value is "P"

a[5] value is "n"

You can also use negative index, where it will start indexing backward, starting at the last character.

a[-1] value is "n"

a[-2] value is "o"

str[starting_index: ending_index] - slicing operator, slices the string at starting index and ends at one character before ending index.

a = "Programming is amazing"

a[0:11] value is "Programming"

a[15:19] value is "amaz"

in - in operator returns True if character is in string.

lang = "language"

"a" in lang, returns True

str.split(char) – Split a string into a list of strings by character char

langs = "Python,C++,C"

langs.split(",") *returns* ['Python', ' C++', 'C']

str.replace(oldval, newval) - replace phrase oldval with newval in string str.

A="Python is powerful"

a.replace("Python", "C++") *returns* 'C++ is powerful'

f-string – is an easy way to format strings and variables, they are easy to use and also faster.

n = 7

print("number is ", n) outputs "number is 7"

print(f"number is {n}") outputs "number is 7"

str.capitalize() - **Capitalize first letter of string, if its already capitalized it returns the original string.**

sent = "message was sent"

sent.capitalize() _returns_ "Message was sent"

str.count(substring) - **returns how many times substring occurs in str.**

mess = "Life is beautiful"

mess.count('is'), returns 1.

str.isalnum() - **returns true if a string is alphanumeric meaning it's a combination of alphabet or/and numbers.**

a = 'door2'

b='door'

c='door#$'

a.isalnum() _return_ True.

b.isalnum() *return* True.

c.isalnum() *return* False.

str.isalpha() – returns True if all string characters are letters.

a = 'door1'

a.isalpha() *returns* False

str.isdigit() - returns True if str contains digits only.

n = '324235'

m = 'd4ds'

n.isdigit(), *returns* True

m.isdigit(), *returns* False

str.islower() - returns True if string characters are all lowercase.

s="People"

s.islower() *return* False

str.isupper() - returns True if string characters are all uppercase.

S = "ALL"

s.isupper() *returns* True.

Python also offer string comparisons operators just as you can compare numbers using ==, >, < etc. You can also compare strings using the same operators.

Operator	name	Description	Example	Returns
==	Equality	Returns True if strings are equal else False.	"Python" == "c++"	False
!=	Not equal	Returns True if strings are not equal else False.	"Python" != "c++"	True
>	Greater than	Returns True if len(str1) > len(str2) else False	"Python" > "c++"	True
>=	Greater than or equal	Returns True if len(str1) => len(str2) else False	"Python" >= "Python"	True
<	Less than	Returns True if len(str1) < len(str2) else False	"Python" < "c++"	False
<=	Less than or equal	Returns True if len(str1) =< len(str2) else False	"Python" <= "c++"	False

Example 1: String methods

The script below uses the string methods we learnt to do interesting operations on strings. This program takes username via input function and do interesting string methods on user name. The code is commented. Read and investigate the code. After you have understood the code, try to tinker with it.

```python
1
2   name = "Nick John"
3
4   n = len(name)
5   index0 = name[0]
6   indexneg = name[-1]
7   index0_4 = name[0:4]
8
9   # Using f-string to concatenate sentences
10  job = f"\'{name} is an Engineer\'"
11  print("using f-string output is", job)
12
13  #slicing and indexing
14  print(f"name length is: {n}")
15  print(f"name index 0 is {index0}")
16  print(f"name index -1 is {indexneg}")
17  print(f"name slice [0:4] is {index0_4}")
18
19  # in operation, split, replace, capitalize
20  is_in = "Nick" in name
21  print(f"\"Nick\" in name returns {is_in}")
22  splited = name.split()
23  print(f"name.split() returns {splited}")
24  name = name.replace("Nick", "Biden")
25  print(f"Nick John after repleacing with name.replace() is {name}")
26  print(f"james captalized is {'james'.capitalize()}")
27
28
29  # count, isalnum, isalpha, isdigit
30  name = "Obama Jame"
31  count = name.count("Nick")
32  print(f"Nick occurs {count} times in \'{name}\'")
33
34  non_alphanum = "eoe12#"
35  non_alpha = "23"
36  digit = '223'
37
38  print(f"{non_alphanum} is alphanumeric is {non_alphanum.isalnum()}")
39  print(f"{non_alpha} is alphabitical is {non_alpha.isalpha()}")
40  print(f"{digit} is only digits {digit.isdigit()}")
41
42
43
44
```

Output:

```
using f-string output is 'Nick John is an Engineer'
name length is: 9
name index 0 is N
name index -1 is n
name slice [0:4] is Nick
"Nick" in name returns True
name.split() returns ['Nick', 'John']
Nick John after repleacing with name.replace() is Biden John
james captalized is James
Nick occurs 0 times in 'Obama Jame'
eoe12# is alphanumeric is False
23 is alphabitical is False
223 is only digits True
```

Example 2 – Reversing name

In this program, we will input our name through input function and the function will print the name length and the reverse of your name. First, we loop through name characters and print each character. For the reverse part, we loop through 1 and up to string length and index the name string using negative i starting backward. For example, if word length is 10, we start with index -1 through -10.

Note: print(char, end='.') prints char and end with '.'
Instead of usual newline.

```
1  name = input("Enter your name: ")
2
3  n = len(name)
4  print("The length of your name is ", n)
5  print()
6  for char in name :
7      print(char,end='.')
8
9  print()
10 print("The reverse is")
11
12 for i in range(1, n+1):
13     print(name[-i], end=".")
```

```
Enter your name: James Bond
The length of your name is  10

J.a.m.e.s. .B.o.n.d.
The reverse is
d.n.o.B. .s.e.m.a.J.
```

Example 3 – Vowels counter program

This program counts the vowels in a string. It starts
by initializing count to zero, then converting all text
characters to lowercase so we can use comparison
between text characters and vowels characters in
lowercase. Then we loop through characters in text

and check if char in vowels, if true count gets incremented by one.

```
1  vowels = 'aeiou'
2
3  # returns the count of vowels in text
4  def count_vowels(text):
5      count = 0
6      # convert text to all lowercase so it compares correctly
7      # to vowels
8      text = text.lower()
9      for char in text:
10          if char in vowels:
11              count += 1
12      return count
13
14  text = "Learning programming is amazing tool to learn"
15  count = count_vowels(text)
16  print(f"There are {count} vowels in text.")
```

There are 15 vowels in text.

Example 4 – Remove negative words from a text

This program iterates through the words by splitting them first using str.split().

str.split() splits negative_words by space into words. For example "I like CS".split() returns ["I", "like", "CS"].The block function loop through negative_words list and if any word is in the text, we replace the word with asterisk string that math negative word length .

```
1  # replace all instances negative words with stars matching the legnth of these words
2
3  negative_words = "bad kill haters"
4
5  def block(text):
6      # split words into list of words
7      for negative in negative_words.split():
8          if negative in text:
9              text = text.replace(negative, len(negative)*'*')
10     return text
11
12 text = "haters kill love"
13 blocked_text = block(text)
14
15 print(f"Original text : {text}")
16 print(f"Blocked text : {blocked_text}")
```

```
Original text : haters kill love
Blocked text : ****** **** love
```

Practice Problems

1. Palindrome is a word which reads the same forward as backward, such as Civic, Level, Mom, Noon and radar. Write a program that return true if the phrase is a palindrome.

2. Write a program that prints how many one-character repeats are there in a given text.

3. Write a program that generate random n length alphanumeric password.

4. Write a program to replace comma with dots in given string, such as "32,323,23" to "32.323.23"

5. Write a program that computes sum of digits in a string, such as "452" digits sum to 11.

Doing Math with Python

Python is a great programming language to perform and analyze data from users. We'll go over a few functions that help you get familiar with python.

Now, this section is not for everyone. It's for those who are interested in implementing a math in their programs, or like math and would like to see it implemented in Python. Some of the concepts are taught in high schools, so this section may not be good for younger students.

int/float

int – Takes string variable and return an integer or if passed with a float returns the integer part of float.

float – Takes string variable and converts it to float number.

Let's look at an example below.

In this example, we put 3 of the numbers through int and float and see the output.

```
1  xi = int(5.2)
2  yi = int(5)
3  zi = int("5")
4  xf = float("5.2")
5  yf = flpat(5.01)
6  zf = float(5)
7
8  print(f"xi is {xi} and it's type is {type(xi)}")
9  print(f"yi is {yi} and it's type is {type(yi)}")
10 print(f"zi is {zi} and it's type is {type(zi)}")
11 print(f"xf is {xf} and it's type is {type(xf)}")
12 print(f"yf is {yf} and it's type is {type(yf)}")
13 print(f"zf is {zf} and it's type is {type(zf)}")
```

Output:

We can see in the output the difference between int and float. We can see that passing a string int i.e. "5" to int function returns int type. Similarly, for float function it takes string that is float i.e. "5.2" and return float number. Note that "5" and "5.2" are strings because they are in quotes. We cannot use them in any mathematical information without using int or float to convert them into numbers.

```
xi is 5 and it's type is <class 'int'>
yi is 5 and it's type is <class 'int'>
zi is 5 and it's type is <class 'int'>
xf is 5.2 and it's type is <class 'float'>
yf is 5.01 and it's type is <class 'float'>
zf is 5.0 and it's type is <class 'float'>
```

We also note that for all values int remove the decimal part and keeps integer part. It does not round up or down, just removes the decimal part.

float retains decimal part. So, use float to convert decimal numbers in strings into actual float numbers.

Rounding numbers – math.ceil(), math.floor() and round()

Python has a built in library called math, it includes a variety of useful mathematical functions.

To access a library in python you must import it first so the main program can have access to a library function.

Next, let's talk about rounding numbers. We use the functions math.ceil(), math.floor() and math.round(). math.ceil() rounds to first integer more than the decimal number , math.floor() rounds to first integer less than the decimal number and round() to the nearest integer (whether it's more or less). Let's look at a sample program.

```python
1  # import the library
2  import math
3  |
4  xc = math.ceil(5.2)
5  yc = math.ceil(7.8)
6  zc = math.ceil(4.5)
7
8  xf = math.floor(5.2)
9  yf = math.floor(7.8)
10 zf = math.floor(4.5)
11
12 xr = round(5.2)
13 yr = round(7.8)
14 zr = round(4.5)
15
16 print(f"Example of math.ceil()")
17 print(f"xc is {xc}")
18 print(f"yc is {yc}")
19 print(f"zc is {zc}")
20 print()
21 print(f"Example of math.floor()")
22 print(f"xf is {xf}")
23 print(f"yf is {yf}")
24 print(f"zf is {zf}")
25 print()
26 print(f"Example of round()")
27 print(f"xr is {xr}")
28 print(f"yr is {yr}")
29 print(f"zr is {zr}")
```

```
Example of math.ceil()
xc is 6
yc is 8
zc is 5

Example of math.floor()
xf is 5
yf is 7
zf is 4

Example of round()
xr is 5
yr is 8
zr is 4
```

```
1  n1 = float(input('num1: '))
2  n2 = float(input('num2: '))
3
4  Sum = n1 + n2
5  difference = n1 - n2
6  product = n1 * n2
7  quotinet = n1/n2
8
9  print()
10 print(f"The sum is {Sum}")
11 print(f"The difference is {difference}")
12 print(f"The product is {product}")
13 print(f"The quotinet is {quotinet}")
```

Add, subtract, multiply, divide

It might seem self-explanatory, but because of how vital it is to do any basic calculation, I will go over the 4 basic mathematical operations.

In this code, we accept two numbers using a python input() function. The two numbers are assigned to two variables n1 and n2.

Then we calculate the sum, difference, product and quotient and assign them to 4 different variables. At the end, these 4 variables are printed out using print().

Output:

```
num1: 9
num2: 3

The sum is 12.0
The difference is 6.0
The product is 27.0
The quotinet is 3.0
```

Modulus operation

The modulus operation returns the remainder between two numbers. It looks like the percentage sign %. Here's an example below:

```
1  n1 = float(input('num1: '))
2  n2 = float(input('num2: '))
3
4  remainder = n1 % n2
5  print()
6  print(f"Remainder is {remainder}")
```

The above code takes in two numbers via an input and finds the remainder between the two; as shown in output below.

Output:

```
num1:  9
num2:  2

Remainder is 1.0
```

The remainder when 9 is divided be 2 is indeed 1.

math.random()

math.random() returns a random number between 0 and 1. If we want to get a random between 0 and 10, we multiply by 10 and round the answer (using math.round()). Let's look at a few examples.

```
1  import random
2
3  n1 = random.random()
4  n2 = round(random.random() * 50)
5  n3 = round(random.random() * 50)
6  n4 = round(random.random() * 1000)
7
8  print(f"Random number between 0 and 1 {n1}")
9  print(f"1st random number between 0 and 50 {n2}")
10 print(f"2nd random number between 0 and 50 {n3}")
11 print(f"Random number between 0 and 1000 {n4}")
```

In the above example, n1 is a random number between 0 and 1. n2 and n3 are two different random numbers between 0 and 50. You should probably see that n2 and n3 are different because both numbers are randomized.

n4 returns a random number between 0 and 1000. We can see the results in the output below. As the numbers are randomized, we should get a different result each time we run the program. math.random() is a fun function and we are going to be using it in quite a few games this book.

Output:

```
Random number between 0 and 1 0.2054234851201563
1st random number between 0 and 50 3
2nd random number between 0 and 50 37
Random number between 0 and 1000 57
```

Exponent and Logarithms

Exponents in python are done using the pow(b, n) or b**n function and logarithm using math.log(n, base). So natural logarithm is done using math.log(number, math.e). If we want logarithm to the base10 we use math.log(n, 10). math.e is Euler constant.

```
1  import math
2
3  n1 = 6 ** 2
4  n2 = 7 ** 3
5  n3 = pow(7, 3)
6  n4 = math.log(100, math.e)
7  n5 = math.log(100, 10)
8
9  print(f"6 raised to the power 2 = {n1}")
10 print(f"7 raised to the power 3 = {n2}")
11 print(f"7 raised to the power 3 = {n3}")
12 print(f"The natural logarithm of 100 is {n4}")
13 print(f"Logarithm base 10 of 100 is {n5}")
```

In the code above, we have three examples of exponents using both ** operator and pow(a, b) function. Basically, x is raised to the power of y in those cases. n1, n2 and n3 give exponents. N4 shows a natural logarithm of 100 and n4 shows logarithm to base 10 of 100.

Output:

```
6 raised to the power 2 = 36
7 raised to the power 3 = 343
7 raised to the power 3 = 343
The natural logarithm of 100 is 4.605170185988092
Logarithm base 10 of 100 is 2.0
```

Square root

math.sqrt() is used the find square root and math.abs() is used to find the absolute value of a number.

Note: You can also use operator ** to find square root by raising number to power 0.5.

Here's a few examples:

```
1  import math
2
3  n1 = 36 ** 0.5
4  n2 = 75 ** 0.5
5  n3 = math.sqrt(75)
6  n4 = abs(13)
7  n5 = abs(-14)
8
9  print(f"The square root of 36 = {n1}")
10 print(f"The square root of 75 = {n2}")
11 print(f"The square root of 75 = {n3}")
12 print(f"The absolute value of 13 = {n4}")
13 print(f"The absolute value of -14 = {n5}")
14
```

In the above code, n1, n2 and n3 are examples of the square root function; while n4 and n5 are examples of the absolute function.

If you haven't heard of the absolute value function, it basically returns a

positive value whether the number is +ve or -ve. So, 13 and -13 would both return an absolute value of 13.

Output:

```
The square root of 36 = 6.0
The square root of 75 = 8.660254037844387
The square root of 75 = 8.660254037844387
The absolute value of 13 = 13
The absolute value of -18 = 14
```

Trigonometry

Yes, Python can be used to do trigonometric functions as well. Here's a few of them. math.sin(x) returns the sine value of x radians. If we want to find the sine of x degrees, then we have to convert it to radians. So, we should change the function to math.sin(x*math.pi/180).

Also, keep in mind that in python, we represent the value of π as math.pi We can also do cos and tan function using math.cos(x) and math.tan(x), where x is in radians. Let's look at an example program below:

```
1   import math
2
3   n1 = math.sin(5)
4   n2 = math.sin(5 * math.pi/180)
5   n3 = math.sin(90 * math.pi/180)
6   n4 = math.cos(10)
7   n5 = math.cos(10 * math.pi/180)
8   n6 = math.cos(0 * math.pi/180)
9   n7 = math.tan(30)
10  n8 = math.tan(30 * math.pi/180)
11  n9 = math.tan(45 * math.pi/180)
12
13  print(f"The sine of 5 radians = {n1}")
14  print(f"The sine of 5 degrees = {n2}")
15  print(f"The sine of 90 degrees = {n3}")
16  print(f"The cosine of 10 radians = {n4}")
17  print(f"The cosine of 10 degrees = {n5}")
18  print(f"The cosine of 0 degrees = {n6}")
19  print(f"The tan of 30 radians = {n7}")
20  print(f"The tan of 30 degrees = {n8}")
21  print(f"The tan of 45 degrees = {n9}")
22
```

In the above code, we show 3 examples of sine, cos and tan values. And we show the difference between calculating trigonometric values of degrees and radians. For example, for n1, we calculate the value of sin(5 radians) and in n2 we calculate the value of sin(5 degrees). In n2, we had to convert 5 degrees into radians by doing sin(5* π/180).

Output:

```
The sine of 5 radians = -0.9589242746631385
The sine of 5 degrees = 0.08715574274765817
The sine of 90 degrees = 1.0
The cosine of 10 radians = -0.8390715290764524
The cosine of 10 degrees = 0.984807753012208
The cosine of 0 degrees = 1.0
The tan of 30 radians = -6.405331196646276
The tan of 30 degrees = 0.5773502691896257
The tan of 45 degrees = 0.9999999999999999
```

Practice Problems

1. Write a program that calculate the salary of an employee. The program takes via input employee hourly rate and the total hours he worked in a month. Don't forget that input function outputs a string input and you need to parse the input to float. Use round function to round salary into 2 decimal numbers.

2. Write a calculator where you ask the user for 2 numbers and calculation operation symbol *, /,+,^,%,log, square root, trig functions. Note that

some of these operations require only one number so modify program behavior accordingly.

3. Create a program that calculates building height H given the distance D from building and the angle α to the tip of a building.

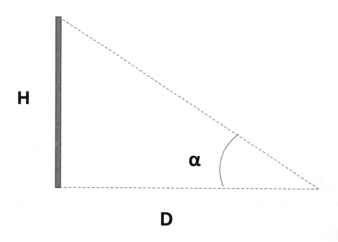

Conditionals and functions

Boolean values and expressions

Python has types int and float for numbers. Similarly, it has type bool for conditional values True and False. Bool is named after British mathematician George Boole who founded the mathematical discipline Boolean algebra, the basis of modern computer science.

Bool types are extremely important in Python because they are used to evaluate conditional statements. Conditional statements are statements that change behavior of program based on some condition.

```
1  print(type(True))
2  print(type(False))
3  print(type(true))

<class 'bool'>
<class 'bool'>

---------------------------------------------------------------------
NameError                              Traceback (most recent call last)
<ipython-input-34-5bfe175a5f35> in <module>
      1 print(type(True))
      2 print(type(False))
----> 3 print(type(true))

NameError: name 'true' is not defined
```

In this snippet, we print out type of True and False. Note that True is not the same as true as the code outputs an error when trying print the type of true instead of True. Boolean expressions are expressions evaluated to either True or False. We write Boolean expression using comparisons operators.

Comparisons operators

Comparison operators are used to compare value in python. Their output is always of type bool either True or False.

Operator	name	Description	Example	Returns
==	Equality	Returns True if numbers are equal else False.	5 == 9	False
!=	Not equal	Returns True if numbers are not equal else False.	5 != 9	True
>	Greater than	Returns True if n1 > n2 else False	10 > 1	True
>=	Greater than or equal	Returns True if n1 => n2 else False	10 >= 10	True
<	Less than	Returns True if n1 < n2 else False	5 < 10	False
<=	Less than or equal	Returns True if n1 =< n2 else False	1 <= 2	False

Logical operators

Python has three logical operators <u>and</u>, <u>or</u> and <u>not</u>. What each one does is similar to their intuitive meaning. The truth table below capture what they do exactly.

X	Y	not x	X or Y	X and Y
True	True	False	True	True
True	False	False	True	False
False	True	True	True	False
False	False	True	False	False

Example 1: Comparisons and logical operators

This snippet illustrates some examples using comparison and logical operators.

```
1   # comparison operators
2
3   x = 0
4   y = 10
5
6   # number comparisons
7   print("y == x is", y == x)
8   print("y >= x is", y >= x)
9   print("y < x is", y < x)
10  print("y <= x is", y <= x)
11
12  print()
13
14  # logical operators
15  print("(not True is)", not True)
16  print("(True and True) is", True and True)
17  print("(True and False) is", True and False)
18  print("(True or False) is", True or False)
19  print("(False or False) is", False or False)
20
21
```

```
y == x is False
y >= x is True
y < x is False
y <= x is False

(not True is) False
(True and True) is True
(True and False) is False
(True or False) is True
(False or False) is False
```

Conditional statements

If conditional

Conditional statement is what makes programs smart. A computer is able to make decisions that enable program to change its behavior according to some Boolean expression that evaluated to either True or False. if conditional in its simplest form is:

If expression:

    statement

Where it executes statement if expression evaluated to True only. Note that statements must be is indented below the if statement. The indented space is called block.

If else conditional

If else is very similar to if conditional except that we have else block that executes if expression is False.

If expression:

    statement1

else:

    statement2

Now we have 2 branches, first branch is statement 1 and second branch is statement 2. The program will execute the branch that correspond to logical expression evaluation. Think of branches as a road that forks into different roads.

if elif else conditional

What if want to have multiple branches instead of only two? if elif else conditional is also called chained conditionals. In chained conditional only one branch is executed. elif stand for else if. We can have any number of elif statements as the program logic needs.

First, if expression is evaluated, if it evaluates to false, then program proceed to evaluating expresion2 belonging to first elif, the program keeps evaluating each expression until it evaluates to True and execute the corresponding statement/block. If all statements evaluate to False then it executes else block.

If expression:

  statement1

```
elif expression2:
        statement2
elif expression2:
        statement3
else:
        statement4
```

Nested Conditional

What if we want to create branches inside other branches? We can nest if conditional inside other if conditional. This is called nested conditional. Keep in mind that too many nested conditionals generally make the program difficult to read so use them only when you can't capture you program logic using combination of logical operators.

```
If expression:
        If expression1:
                statement1
        else:
                statement2
```

else:

    statement3

```
1  x = -1
2  y = 5
3
4  # nested conditional
5  if x < 0 :
6      if y < 10:
7          print("nested conditional: x < 0 and y < 10")
8
9  print()
10 # Equivale version using and
11 if x < 0 and y < 10:
12     print("and version conditional: x < 0 and y < 10")
```

nested conditional: x < 0 and y < 10

and version conditional: x < 0 and y < 10

In this snippet, nested conditional was reduced into a flat if conditional using "and" logical operators. Observe that the second if conditional is easier to read.

Example 2: Conditionals:

In this program, we first check if x is a positive number using simple if conditional. Check if y is positive or negative number using if else conditional. Note that there is a corner case left unchecked when y is zero so we use if elif else to check if z is positive, negative or zero.

```
1  # simple if case
2  x = 5
3  y = -3
4  z = 0
5
6  # only check for positivity
7  if x > 0 :
8      print("x is positive number !")
9
10 print()
11
12 # Check if number is positive or negative using if else
13 if y > 0 :
14     print("y is positive number !")
15 else :
16     print("y is positive number !")
17
18 print()
19
20 # Check if number is positive, negative or zero using if elif else
21 if z > 0 :
22     print("z is positive number !")
23 elif z < 0 :
24     print("z is positive number !")
25 else:
26     print("z is zero !", z)
```

```
x is positive number !

y is positive number !

z is zero 0
```

Functions

A function is a block of reusable code that performs specific task when called. Think of them as a machine/black box which take inputs and transform them into outputs. This black box is run every time it's called. Functions help in breaking the code into simple easily maintainable reusable modules. In fact, you have been using function all the way through this book without noticing. For example, print() is a function that takes string input and display it on screen. Also, the string methods you learnt in the past chapter are function that operates on strings.

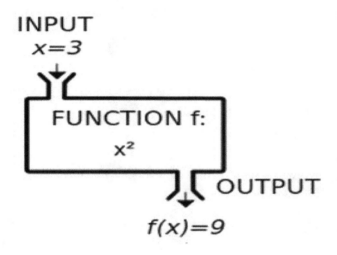

A black box representing square function

Functions definition

Functions are defined in python using def keyword.

def function_name(input_ parameters):

    statements

to call a function type the function name with inputs.

function_name(input_ parameters)

In the code below, we define a function that great a user by name. It takes one input a name and print hello to user name.

```
1  # function example
2  my_name = 'Jame'
3
4  # say hello to name
5  def hello(name):
6      print("Hello !", name)
7
8  # function call
9  hello(my_name)
```

Hello ! Jame

return statement

In the previous script, we ran print function inside hello function, but what if we need to return just a value instead to the caller?

In this snippet, hello function returns a string. hello function is called first and the returned value is stored in the assigned variable.

```
 1  # function example
 2  my_name = 'Jame'
 3
 4  # return hello to name
 5  def hello(name):
 6      return "Hello !" + name
 7
 8  # function call
 9  retruned_name = hello(my_name)
10  print(retruned_name)
```

```
Hello !Jame
```

Empty return

When a function return statement is empty it terminates the function run and return None.

In this example when func is called it only execute line 4 because it terminates when it reaches return statement at line 5. Also, note that it returns None value.

```
 1  # None return|
 2
 3  def func():
 4      print("Before return nothing")
 5      return
 6      print("After return nothing")
 7
 8  m = func()
 9  print()
10  print("func returned ", m)
```

```
before return nothing

func returned  None
```

Example 3: is divisible:

In this example, is_divisible function checks if a is divisible by b, if so, it prints a message and set div to true. If a is not divisible by b, else statement will handle this case where it prints message and set div to false.

```
1   # is divisible
2
3   # checks if a is divisible by b, print a massage
4   # return true if divisible else false
5
6   def is_divisible(a, b):
7
8       div = None
9       if a % b == 0 :
10          print(f"{a} is divisible by {b}")
11          div = True
12      else:
13          print(f"{a} is not divisible by {b}")
14          div = False
15
16      return div
17
18  n1 = is_divisible(8, 2)
19  n2 = is_divisible(8, 3)
20
21  print(n1)
22  print(n2)
```

```
8 is divisible by 2
8 is not divisible by 3
True
False
```

Practice Problems

1. Write a program that finds numbers divisible by 11 between 1 and 5000.

2. Write a function that test if a number is a prime number. Prime numbers are number divisible only by itself and 1.

3. Write a function that tests if number is odd.

Loops

Loops in coding are a sequence of instructions that are repeated a certain number of times.

Think of a loop like repeating operation that keeps repeating until a condition is met.

There are mainly 2 types of loops based on the conditions of execution. They are:

a. **FOR Loops:** FOR loops contain a sequence of instructions that are executed for a certain number of times. For example, a FOR loop from 1 to 10 executes the code inside the loop 10 times.
b. **WHILE Loops**: WHILE loops is a sequence of instructions that are executed till a certain condition is met.

Now, if we want to do a 1000 executions of execute function; we use a FOR loop. The FOR loop below starts at 0 and ends at 999, thus running execute function 1000 times.

```
for i in range(1000):
    Execute()
```

Finally, if we want to keep running execute() till 6 PM, we use a WHILE loop.

```
While (checktime!= 18:00):
    Execute();
```

These are simple examples of the loops to explain the concepts of loops. This concept is very important in coding.

Now, let's do some examples in python.

FOR LOOP Example 1

A simple example of a For Loop is a program that counts to 10.

```
1  for i in range(11):
2      print(i)
```

The above code is probably the simplest example of a for loop. The loop runs from 0 to 10 so it runs 11 times each time printing i which is the loop iteration number.

Note: range(n) function makes the loop runs from 0 to n-1.

for i in range(11)

The line above means that the loop starts from 0 (i=0). It is increasing by 1 each time. The loop ends when i reaches 10.

Output:

```
0
1
2
3
4
5
6
7
8
9
10
```

You can see the numbers 0 to 10 printed on the screen.

FOR LOOP Example 2

Now, let's do a slightly different version of this. In this example, we're going to use an input that takes in a number for the loop. That means we can make the loop as long as we want.

```
1  loop_length = int(input("Please enter the loop length: "))
2
3  for i in range(loop_length):
4      print(i)
```

The input takes in a number input and stores in a variable called "loop_length".

The loop prints all the numbers between 0 and "loop_length" variable. In the example below, we put 15 in input; and as we can see, it prints out numbers between 0 and 14. Note that loop stops right before n because python starts indexing at 0 and up to but not including "loop_length" .

```
Please enter the loop length: 15
0
1
2
3
4
5
6
7
8
9
10
11
12
13
14
```

FOR Loop Example 3 – Nested Loops

In this final example, we use FOR loops to create a star a half pyramid pattern. The program asks for a pyramid length and stores it in a variable called pyramid_height.

Then it runs 2 nested loops where the outer loop iterates for the pyramid 'levels' and the inner loop prints the stars at each level starting from zero. Each level contains j stars where j is the current level number.

So, for example, if you're going through the first loop for the 5th time, i=5. The second loop prints * from 0 to 4 (i.e. 5 times).

In the example, below, we print a half pyramid for a pyramid_height of 8.

```
1   pyramid_height = int(input("Please enter the pyramid height: "))
2
3
4   for i in range(pyramid_height):
5       for j in range(i):
6           print('*', end='')
7       print()
```

```
Please enter the pyramid height: 8

*
**
***
****
*****
******
*******
```

WHILE LOOP EXAMPLE 1

A while loop runs while a certain condition is met. If the condition is no longer met, it breaks out of the loop. In the below example, the program executes a while loop that takes in a user input via the input function. The while loop keeps running and printing the user text. The loop stops when the user inputs the word 'STOP'. Once the word is input, that's the end of the while loops and the program stops.

```
1  text = ''
2
3  while(text != 'stop'):
4      text = input("What do you want to do now ? ")
5      print("Activity is :", text)
```

Output:

```
What do you want to do now ? Read
Activity is : Read
What do you want to do now ? play
Activity is : play
What do you want to do now ? study
Activity is : study
What do you want to do now ? stop
Activity is : stop
```

We can see while loop kept asking the user for an input until the user entered "stop", the while loop condition was met and it ceased execution.

Practice Problems

1. Write a program that takes 2 inputs numbers a and b and return the remainder of a divided by b.

2. Write a program that outputs a number multiplication table up to 10.

For example, if 3 is entered it outputs:

3, 6, 9, 12, 15, 18, 21, 24, 27, 30

3. Write a program that find the length of given word using a for loop. Note: python already have len() function that return the length of a string, try to use both , a loop and len() .

4. Write a program that that counts the total number of digits in number. For example, "345abcd32" has 5 digits.

5. Write a program that keeps taking user input number until an even number is entered where it stops.

6. Write a program that takes two numbers a and b then it outputs all odd numbers between a and b inclusive.

7. Write a program that takes a user input pyramid height and outputs the following symmetrical pyramid pattern. For example, if the user inputs the number '5' then the pattern is:

```
   *
  **
 ****
******
********
```

8. Write a program that sums all numbers from 1 up to n where n is a number that the user input. Note: First approach this problem using for loop then use the formula $1 + 2 + \ldots + n = n(n+1) / 2$.

Gaming Time - Loops

Now, it's time to design a few games based on what we've learned so far. There's no better way of learning concepts than applying them; and even better to apply them to something fun.

Game 1 – Guess Random Numbers

In this game, we're going to create a program that takes in a number via Input function. The number is between 0 and 10. Then we compare that number to a random number generated via random module (using random.randint). If it is the same, then the guessed number is correct. If not, then we give them the right number. See the code and output below.

```
1  import random
2
3  print("You have only three tries to guesss number correctly")
4
5  # generate random integer between 0 and 10
6  random_number = random.randint(0, 10)
7
8
9  won = False
10 for try_num in range(3):
11     print()
12     print(f"Try number {try_num+1}")
13     guessed_number = int(input("Guess a number between 0 and 10 inclusive: "))
14
15     if(guessed_number == random_number):
16         won = True
17         print("Good job ! You won")
18         break
19     else:
20         print("Incorrect, try again !")
21
22 if(won == False):
23     print()
24     print("You ran out of tries, Good luck next time")
25     print("The right number is ", random_number)
26
```

random.randint(n, m) generates a random number between n and m inclusive this different from random. random() generates random real number anywhere in the range 0 and 1.

This is basically built around a for loop which runs 3 times giving the user 3 tries to guess the random number correctly. If the user guesses the random number correctly then, **if** block, at line 15 will set the **won** variable to **True** and break out of the loop. In python to break out of the loop we use "break". The **if** block at line number 22 is used when the user has run out of his tries.

Output:

```
You have only three tries to guesss number correctly

Try number 1
Guess a number between 0 and 10 inclusive: 4
Incorrect, try again !

Try number 2
Guess a number between 0 and 10 inclusive: 4
Incorrect, try again !

Try number 3
Guess a number between 0 and 10 inclusive: 5
Incorrect, try again !

You ran out of tries, Good luck next time
The right number is  9
```

If the user wins here is a sample output:

```
You have only three tries to guesss number correctly

Try number 1
Guess a number between 0 and 10 inclusive: 5
Good job ! You won
```

This program is a good way to practice conditional loops and random number generators.

Game 2 – Math Quiz Game

This program prints out 5 simple math problems and takes in answers to these problems via input they are (user_ans1, user_ans2, user_ans3, user_ans4, user_ans5). The answers are stored in variables as (ans1, ans2, ans3, ans4, ans5). These answers are compared to the real answers using if conditional. A counter score is incremented by 1 each time the user gets a correct answer and finally the counter is printed to see how many correct answers the user gets.

```
1   # Game 2 - Math Quiz Game
2
3   print("This is a game where you find basic mathmatical operations for 2 integer numbers n1 and n2 \n")
4   n1 = 8
5   n2 = 2
6
7   ans1 = n1 + n2
8   ans2 = n1 - n2
9   ans3 = n1 * n2
10  ans4 = n1 % n2
11
12  user_ans1 = int(input(f"{n1} + {n2} = "))
13  user_ans2 = int(input(f"{n1} - {n2} = "))
14  user_ans3 = int(input(f"{n1} * {n2} = "))
15  user_ans4 = int(input(f"{n1} % {n2} = "))
16  print()
17
18  score = 0
19
20  if ans1 == user_ans1:
21      score += 1
22  if ans2 == user_ans2:
23      score += 1
24  if ans3 == user_ans3:
25      score += 1
26  if ans4 == user_ans4:
27      score += 1
28
29  print(f'You have got {score} answers correct')
```

Output:

`8 + 2 =` [   ]

This is a game where you find basic mathmatical operations for 2 integer numbers n1 and n2

The game keeps asking for input for the 4 questions here is the final output after all answers are entered.

```
This is a game where you find basic mathmatical operations for 2 integer numbers n1 and n2

8 + 2 = 10
8 - 2 = 6
8 * 2 = 16
8 % 2 = 0

You have got 4 answers correct
```

This is a great practice program. But you might be thinking that kids can use this program only once as we always use the same numbers. To fix this problem, we generate random numbers in the next game.

Game 3 – Math Quiz with Random Numbers

In this program below, there are 5 math questions generated by 10 random numbers. The 10 random numbers are variables **n1** through **n10**. The answers to the questions are calculated and are stored in variables **ans1** through **ans5**. These 15 variables are called global variables as they are outside any functions. This means that their values can be accessed anywhere in the program by any function. The function **print_ans()** uses the 5 variables **ans1** through **ans2** to write the quiz answers. These answers **(answer1-answer5)** are checked against user answers **(user_ans1- user_ans5)** using 5 different if conditionals in **check_ans** function. Each time there is a correct answer, a counter is incremented. Eventually, the counter is printed to show the number of correct answers. These questions are randomly generated which means that the user gets different questions each time.

Program

```
1   #Game 3 - Math Quiz with Random Numbers
2
3   import random
4
5   Max_int = 10
6
7   # Assign random integers between 1 and Max_int inclusive
8   n1 = random.randint(1, Max_int)
9   n2 = random.randint(1, Max_int)
10  n3 = random.randint(1, Max_int)
11  n4 = random.randint(1, Max_int)
12  n5 = random.randint(1, Max_int)
13  n6 = random.randint(1, Max_int)
14  n7 = random.randint(1, Max_int)
15  n8 = random.randint(1, Max_int)
16  n9 = random.randint(1, Max_int)
17  n10 = random.randint(1, Max_int)
18
19  ans1 = n1 + n2
20  ans2 = n3 - n4
21  ans3 = n5 * n6
22  ans4 = n7 * n8
23  ans5 = n9 % n10
24
25  user_ans1 = int(input(f"{n1} + {n2} = "))
26  user_ans2 = int(input(f"{n3} - {n4} = "))
27  user_ans3 = int(input(f"{n5} * {n6} = "))
28  user_ans4 = int(input(f"{n7} * {n8} = "))
29  user_ans5 = int(input(f"{n9} % {n10} = "))
30  print()
31
```

```
32  # check answers and find user score
33  def check_ans():
34      score = 0
35      if ans1 == user_ans1:
36          score += 1
37      if ans2 == user_ans2:
38          score += 1
39      if ans3 == user_ans3:
40          score += 1
41      if ans4 == user_ans4:
42          score += 1
43      if ans5 == user_ans5:
44          score += 1
45      return score
46
47  #print user answers
48  def print_ans():
49
50      print("Answer 1 = ", ans1)
51      print("Answer 2 = ", ans2)
52      print("Answer 3 = ", ans3)
53      print("Answer 4 = ", ans4)
54      print("Answer 5 = ", ans5)
55
56
57  # find user score
58  score = check_ans()
59  print_ans()
60  print(f'\nYou have got {score} answers correct.')
```

Output:

```
7 + 6 = 13
7 - 10 = -3
2 * 1 = 2
6 * 2 = 12
2 % 7 = 0

Answer 1 =  13
Answer 2 =  -3
Answer 3 =  2
Answer 4 =  12
Answer 5 =  2

You have got 4 answers correct.
```

Practice Problems

1. Write a program that generates two random numbers between 0 and 10 inclusive. Then it outputs their sum, multiplication, remainder and exponentiation.

2. Write a random password generator, the program takes the password length n from user and it creates n digits long password.

3. Write a program that takes 3 side lengths of a triangle from user and then it finds out whether it is acute, right or obtuse angle triangle (Hint: Use Pythagoras theorem to check).

Lists, tuples and dictionaries

Introduction to data structure

Data structures are structures used to store and group data so they can easily access and manipulate data efficiently .Each type of data structure has its advantages and disadvantages .A specific data structure is selected based on what you want to optimize .There are different aspects to optimize, for example, access speed or storage size or data modification speed. Each of these aspects will require different types of data structure optimized for this aspect.

In this chapter, we will explore three fundamentals built in python data structures. Lists, tuples and dictionaries. These data structures are immensely useful. They make your program easier to write and more efficient and you didn't have to implement your own data structures from scratch. Note that these data structures are also called containers since they hold/contain other objects.

Lists

Lists are sequences that store collections of items. List is one of the containers most commonly used due to its versatility. Lists can hold different types of data. They are heterogeneous meaning they don't have to store similar data types. Lists are mutable so you cany modify a list after its creation.

To create a list, put comma separated value in square brackets.

my_list = []   or

my_list = list( )

The code below creates lists of numbers, strings and a heterogenous list of both numbers and strings.

```
 1  # create list either by square brackets or list()
 2  my_list = []
 3  my_list = list()
 4
 5
 6  # Define list l1, l2, l3
 7  # List1 sequnce of numbers
 8  list1 = [1, 2, 3]
 9
10  # list2 sequence of strings
11  list2 = ["Nick", "Tom", "Jane"]
12
13  # list3 sequence of numbers and strings
14  list3 = ["Nick", 10, "Python", 50]
15
16  # list4 a list containg other lists
17  list4 = [11, 12, 13]
18
19  print("list1 is:", 11)
20  print("list2 is:", 12)
21  print("list3 is:", 13)
22  print("list4 is:", 14)
```

```
list1 is: [1, 2, 3]
list2 is: ['Nick', 'Tom', 'Jane']
list3 is: ['a', 1, 'Python', 5]
list4 is: [[1, 2, 3], ['Nick', 'Tom', 'Jane'], ['a', 1, 'Python', 5]]
```

List methods

Similar to the string methods discussed in earlier
chapters. Lists comes with useful methods to use.
We will study frequently used list methods here, to
find out and learn more methods follow this python
documentation link.

https://docs.python.org/3/tutorial/datastructures.ht
ml

This table summaries basic list operations.

Expression	Name	Output
len(['a', 'b', '1'])	Length	3
['a', 'b', 'c'] + ['d', 'e', 'f']	List concatenation	['a', 'b', 'c', 'd', 'e', 'f']
['hi'] * 4	Repetition	['Hi!', 'Hi!', 'Hi!', 'Hi!']
'a' in ['a', 'b', 'c']	Membership	True
for num in [1, 2, 3]: print(num)	List iteration	1 2 3
n = ['a', 'b', 'c'] n[0] = 'z' print(n)	List element assignment	['z', 'b', 'c']

list[index] – Indexing operator, selects a single value from a list. The number inside the brackets is called index, it is an integer value. Indexing in python starts at zero. Similar to strings you can also have negative index where it starts indexing backward.

list1 = ['Python', 'C++', 'C', 'Java Script']

list1[0] value is 'Python'

list1[2] value is 'C'

list1[-1] value is 'Java Script'

list1[-2] value is 'C'

list[starting_index: ending_index] -
slicing operator, slices the list at starting index and ends at one element before ending index.

list1 = ['Python', 'C++', 'C', 'Java Script']

list1[0:2] = ['Python', 'C++']

list1[0:-1] = ['Python', 'C++', 'C']

list.append(elem) – *Append element to list.*

list1 = [1, 2, 3]
list1.append(4)
list1 value is *[1, 2, 3, 4]*

list.clear() – Clears list values .

list1 = [1,2,3]
list1.clear()
list1 value is *[]*

list.count(elem) – Count how many times element elem is on list .

list1 = [1,2,2,2,3,4]

list1.count(2) outputs 3

list.extend(list2) – Adds list2 elements to list .This method performs same job as lists concatenation using '+' operator .

list1 = [1, 2, 3]

list2 = [4, 5]

list1.extend(list2)

list1 is [1,2,3,4,5]

list.insert(elem_index , elem) – Insert element elem into list at index elem_index.

list1 = [1, 2, 3]

list1.insert(3, 4))

list1 is [1,2,3,4]

list.pop( ) – Removes list last element.

list1 = [1, 2, 3, 4]

list1.pop() removes 4

list1 is *[1,2,3]*

list.index(elem) – Returns index of first occurrence of elem.

list1 = [1, 2 , 3, 4]

list1.index(2) returns 3

Example 1: List basic operation

Here we have a comprehensive example to various list methods discussed above. Experiment with the code to understand it.

```
 1  # List basic operations
 2
 3
 4  # List iteration and indexing
 5  even_nums = [0, 2, 4, 6, 8, 10]
 6
 7  # Length of even_nums list
 8  print("Length of even_nums list is:", len(even_nums))
 9  print('\n')
10
11  print("Even numbers are:")
12  for number in even_nums:
13      print(number)
14      |
15  # print 2 new lines, new line symbol is \n
16  print('\n')
17
18  # Slicing
19  # print even number list less than 5
20  even_nums_less_5 = even_nums[0:3]
21  print("Even numbers less than 5 are: ", even_nums_less_5)
22  print('\n')
23
24  # Append additional even number
25  even_nums.append(12)
26  print("Even number list after appending is: ", even_nums)
27  print('\n')
28
29  # count how many times 12 is in list
30  count = even_nums.count(12)
31  print(f"12 occurs {count} times in even_nums list")
32  print('\n')
```

```
32  print('\n')
33
34
35  # clear list values
36  even_nums.clear()
37  print("Even number list after clearing is: ", even_nums)
38  print('\n')
39
40  # extend the empty list
41  even_nums.extend(['Tom', 1, 'python'])
42  print("Even number list after extending is: ", even_nums)
43  print('\n')
44
45  # insert new element at index 0
46  even_nums.insert(0, 'new')
47  print("Even number list after inserting at index 0 is: ", even_nums)
48  print('\n')
49
50  # pop list last element
51  even_nums.pop()
52  print("Even number list after popping is: ", even_nums)
53  print('\n')
54
55
56  # find the index of 'Tom' and change it to Nick
57  index_python = even_nums.index('Tom')
58  even_nums[index_python] = 'Nick'
59
60  print("Even number after replacing Tom is: ", even_nums)
```

Output:

```
Length of even_nums list is: 6

Even numbers are:
0
2
4
6
8
10

Even numbers less than 5 are:  [0, 2, 4]

Even number list after appending is:  [0, 2, 4, 6, 8, 10, 12]

12 occurs 1 times in even_nums list

Even number list after clearing is:  []

Even number list after extending is:  ['Tom', 1, 'python']

Even number list after inserting at index 0 is:  ['new', 'Tom', 1, 'python']

Even number list after popping is:  ['new', 'Tom', 1]

Even number after replacing Tom is:  ['new', 'Nick', 1]
```

Tuples

Tuples are similar to lists as they also store collection of items. In facts tuple can be considered immutable lists. Tuples are immutable, once assigned, they can't change. This makes them more efficient and faster.

103

Tuples are defined using parentheses whereas lists are defines using square brackets.

To create a tuple, put comma separated value in parentheses.

my_tuple = (1,3,5)

For a single value tuple follow the value with a comma. Without a comma python considers it a number.

my_tuple = (1,)

In this snippet we create tuples and try to modify its value, however python throws type error because tuples are immutable.

```
1   # create a tuple
2
3   # single value tuple
4   tu1 = (1, )
5
6   print("Single value tuple: ", tu)
7   # Multi values tuple
8   tu2 = (1, 'a', 'python')
9   print("Multi value tuple: ", tu)
10  print("tuple type is ", type(tu2))
11
12  # try modifying tuple
13  tu[2] = 'C++'
```

```
Single value tuple:  (1, 'a', 'python')
Multi value tuple:  (1, 'a', 'python')
tuple type is  <class 'tuple'>

-----------------------------------------------------------------
TypeError                           Traceback (most recent call last)
<ipython-input-7-a5d65c274c9b> in <module>
     11
     12 # try modifying tuple
---> 13 tu[2] = 'C++'

TypeError: 'tuple' object does not support item assignment
```

Tuples methods

Similar to lists, tuples support basic methods like
indexing, len, slicing and in membership operator.
Tuple also support index and count method. Note
that tuples don't have many methods as lists
because they are immutable.

Example *2*: *Tuple* methods

In this example, we perform basic methods on a tuple. Note that these methods are the same as in list methods.

```
1   # Basic tuple methods|
2   tu = ('Tom', 'Jane', 'Python', 10, 'Tom')
3
4   # Len()
5   print("Tuple length is :", len(tu))
6
7   # Element access
8   print("Last element of tuple is :",tu[-1])
9
10  # slicing
11  print("tu[0:3] is :",tu[0:3])
12
13  # index method
14  print("'Python' is at index:",tu.index('Python'))
15
16  # count method
17  print("'Tom' occurs:",tu.count('Tom'))
18
```

```
Tuple length is : 5
Last element of tuple is : Tom
tu[0:3] is : ('Tom', 'Jane', 'Python')
'Python' is at index: 2
'Tom' occurs: 2
```

Dictionaries

Dictionaries are key value pairs. While lists and tuples are accessed by a position index, dictionary values are accessed by their corresponding key. The keys must be immutable such as strings, numbers or even tuples but not a list as lists are mutable. Keys are also unique you can't have 2 values with the same key.

Dictionaries are defined by comma separate Key: Value pairs in curly brackets.

To create empty dictionary:

my_dict = {}

or

my_list = dict()

To create a basic dictionary:

num_dict = {'one':1, 'two':2, 'three':3}

Basic dictionary methods

To access a dictionary value, use its key.

num_dict = {'one':1, 'two':2, 'three':3}

num_dict['one'] is 1

Membership is similar to tuple and lists except that it checks for key.

num_dict = {'one':1, 'two':2, 'three':3}

'one' in num_dict returns True

To add new key value pair use assignment operator.

num_dict = {'one':1, 'two':2, 'three':3}

num_dict['four'] = 4

num_dict now is {'one':1, 'two':2, 'three':3, 'four':4}

dict.clear – clears the dictionary .

num_dict = {'one':1, 'two':2, 'three':3}

num_dict.clear()

num_dict now is {}

dict.get(key) – retrieve a dictionary value by a key and returns None if no such key exists.

num_dict = {'one':1, 'two':2, 'three':3}

num_dict.get('one') returns 1

dict.pop(key) – removes key:value pair corresponding to key.

num_dict = {'one':1, 'two':2, 'three':3}

num_dict.pop('three') removes 3

num_dict now is {'one':1, 'two':2}

dict.items() – return a list of (key, value) tuples.

num_dict = {'one':1, 'two':2, 'three':3}

num_dict.items() returns [('one', 1), ('two', 2), ('three', 3)]

dict.keys() – returns dict_key object containing all dictionary keys.

num_dict = {'one':1, 'two':2, 'three':3}

num_dict.items() returns dict_key(['one', 'two', 'three'])

dict.values() – returns a list of dictionary values.

num_dict = {'one':1, 'two':2, 'three':3}

num_dict.values() returns [1, 2, 3]

Example *3*: *Dictionary* methods

In example 3, We use and experiment with the dictionary method we learnt.

```python
 1  # create a dictionary of shopping items quantity
 2
 3  shopcart = {'chips':2, 'ink cartridge':1, 'paper':1}
 4
 5  # dictionary length counts key:value pairs
 6  print('Shopcart is:', shopcart)
 7  print('Your shopcart distinct items are ', len(shopcart))
 8  print('\n')
 9
10
11  # shope cart include a pens ?
12  pens_in = 'pens' in shopcart
13
14  # membership test
15  print("There is a pen in shopping car:", pens_in)
16  print('\n')
17
18  # accessing a value
19  print("The number of chips items is", shopcart['chips'])
20  print('\n')
21
22  # add a pair
23  shopcart['orange juice'] = 4
24  print(shopcart)
25  print('\n')
26
27
28  # get method
29  print("Quanattiy of orange juice is", shopcart.get('orange juice'))
30  print('\n')
31
32  # pop method removes element at a key
33  shopcart.pop('paper')
34  print(shopcart)
35  print('\n')
```

```
36
37   # get items, keys, values
38   items = shopcart.items()
39   keys = shopcart.keys()
40   values = shopcart.values()
41
42   print("Shopcart items are:", items)
43   print("Shopcart keys are:", keys)
44   print("Shopcart values are:", values)
```

```
Shopcart is: {'chips': 2, 'ink cartridge': 1, 'paper': 1}
Your shopcart distinct items are  3


There is a pen in shopping car False


The number of chips items is 2


{'chips': 2, 'ink cartridge': 1, 'paper': 1, 'orange juice': 4}


Quanattiy of orange juice is 4


{'chips': 2, 'ink cartridge': 1, 'orange juice': 4}


Shopcart items are: dict_items([('chips', 2), ('ink cartridge', 1), ('orange juice', 4)])
Shopcart keys are: dict_keys(['chips', 'ink cartridge', 'orange juice'])
Shopcart values are: dict_values([2, 1, 4])
```

Example 4 – Guess World Capitals

In this example we use both list and dictionary. A dictionary capital_dict is used to make country:capital key pairs. Then we get the dictionary keys using keys() method and store them in countries list. This is essential so we can use random.choice() function which takes a list and return a value from list randomly. Then inside an infinite while loop, user is asked for a capital using input function and the answer is compared to actual capitals.

```
1   # World capital game
2   import random
3
4   # World capitals dictionary
5   capital_dic={
6       'spain':'madrid',
7       'france':'paris',
8       'germany':'berlin',
9       'norway':'oslo',
10      'india':'new delhi',
11      'egypt':'cairo'
12  }
13
14  # get countries and convert it to list so we can use random function
15  countries = list(capital_dic.keys())
16  print ('Let\'s learn World Capitals. Enter quit to quit the game.')
17
18
19  while True:
20      # pick a random country
21      country = random.choice(countries)
22      capital = capital_dic[country]
23
24      guess = input(f'what is the capital of {country}.')
25      # if user type quit, quit
26      if guess.lower() == 'quit':
27          break
28      elif guess.lower() == capital:
29          print(f'Correct !')
30          break
31      else:
32          print(f'Incorrect. The capital of {country} is {capital}.')
33
```

Output:

what is the capital of india. [   ]

Let's learn World Capitals. Enter quit to quit the game.

Wrong answer is entered.

Let's learn World Capitals. Enter quit to quit the game.
what is the capital of india.cairo
Incorrect. The capital of india is new delhi.

what is the capital of norway. [   ]

Correct answer is entered.

```
Let's learn World Capitals. Enter quit to quit the game.
what is the capital of india.cairo
Incorrect. The capital of india is new delhi.
what is the capital of norway.oslo
Correct !
```

In above code, Cairo is entered as the capital of India. As the answer is incorrect, the program outputs 'Incorrect. The capital of india is new delhi'.

In the second part of the program, 'oslo' is entered as the correct capital of Norway, and the program outputs 'correct!'

Example 5 – Random quotes

This example generates random quote from a tuple of quotes using random.choice() function. While a list would also work, a tuple is used because we never intend to manipulate quotes, they remain immutable throughout the program. For large immutable object, tuple is more efficient and also secures since it guarantees that object can never change without having error. Preventing accidental manipulation.

```
 1   # Random quote
 2   import random
 3
 4   # since we dont intend to do any operation on quotes we use tuple instead of lists
 5   quotes = (
 6       "Yesterday's the past, tomorrow's the future, but today is a gift.",
 7       "The best preparation for tomorrow is doing your best today.",
 8       "Change your life today.",
 9       "If you fell down yesterday, stand up today.",
10       "Never give up. ",
11       "Dream as if you'll live forever.",
12       "The science of today is the technology of tomorrow.",
13       "Did I offer peace today?",
14   )
15
16   rand_quotes = random.choice(quotes)
17   print("Todays quote is:", rand_quotes)
18
```

Todays quote is: Change your life today.

Example 6 – Guess a country name

In this example, we make a game similar to hangman where we ask the user to guess the name of the country. We have a tuple of various country names. The user is allowed to have guess a few times incorrectly before losing. We make a list of correctly guessed characters where correct guesses are appended to. The user wins when the guessed list length is equal to country name length.

Note that we used a list data structure for guessed characters since it is continuously updated while countries are in tuple since it is never mutated.

```
1  # guess a random country
2
3  import random
4
5  # list of countries
6  countries = ('france', 'usa', 'spain', 'india', 'brazil', 'norway', 'germany')
7
8  # Choose random country from countries
9  country = random.choice(countries)
10
11 # number of turns
12 turns = 4
13
14 # a list to store the guessed characters
15 guessed = []
16 while turns > 0:
17
18     # print guessed characters
19     for char in country:
20         if char in guessed:
21             print(char, end='')
22         else:
23             print('-', end='')
24
25     print()
26     print(f"You have {turns} left.")
27
28     # user input
29     guess = input("guess a character:")
30
31     # make sure guess is lowercase
32     guess.lower()
```

```
33
34        # if guess already made
35        if guess in guessed :
36            print("You have already made this guess\n")
37
38        # check input with the character in word
39        if guess not in country:
40            turns -= 1
41        else:
42            # character is in word , append character
43            # the number of times it appear in word
44            count = country.count(guess)
45            for i in range(count):
46                guessed.append(guess)
47
48        # if guessed length match country length then user wins
49        # else if ran out of turns user loses
50        if len(guessed) == len(country):
51            print("Congratulation you guessed correctly!!")
52            break
53        elif turns == 0 :
54            print("Good luck next time")
55
56
57
58
```

Output:

```
Guess the characters
------
You have 4 left.
guess a character:n
n-----
You have 4 left.
guess a character:o
no----
You have 4 left.
guess a character:r
nor---
You have 4 left.
guess a character:w
norw--
You have 4 left.
guess a character:a
norwa-
You have 4 left.
guess a character:f
norwa-
You have 3 left.
guess a character:y
Congratulation you guessed correctly!!
```

Practice Problems

1. Write a program to append all dictionary values to a list.

2. Write a program to check if a given key exist in a dictionary.

3. Write a program to find highest numerical value in a dictionary.

4. Write a program that takes 2 equally sized lists and convert them into a dictionary where list 1 contains the keys and list 2 contains the values.

5. Create a program that picks and prints a random joke from list or tuple of jokes .

Objects

Objects

An object is a collection of instances of data structures that belong to a class. These instances can have different data types. Think of a class as a factory that produce objects.

Example 1: Object Shape

In this example. We create a class shape, the class assigns name, color, size and position to object. Then we create object my_shape by calling the class at line 8.

At line 9 through 12, we access object values by using dot '.' notation. For example, my_shape.name is circle.

Then we change object values by reassigning them to different values.

```
1  # create class
2  class shape:
3      name = 'circle'
4      color = 'red'
5      size = 5
6      position = (0,0)
7
8  my_shape = shape()
9  print("name is: ", my_shape.name)
10 print("color is: ", my_shape.color)
11 print("size is: ", my_shape.size)
12 print("position is: ", my_shape.position)
13
14 my_shape.name = 'triangle'
15 my_shape.color = 'black'
16 my_shape.size = 10
17 my_shape.position = (10, 10)
18
19 print()
20 print("my_shape values after reassignment are:")
21 print()
22
23 print("name is: ", my_shape.name)
24 print("color is: ", my_shape.color)
25 print("size is: ", my_shape.size)
26 print("position is: ", my_shape.position)
27
```

```
name is:  circle
color is:  red
size is:  5
position is:  (0, 0)

my_shape values after reassignment are:

name is:  triangle
color is:  black
size is:  10
position is:  (10, 10)
```

Example 2: Dice Game

This is a game of dice between 2 players where dice is flipped 1000 times. If dice flip result in an even number player 1 wins one point, if it is odd player 2 wins 1 point. The dice flip is implemented using random number function randint which generate numbers between 1 and 6 inclusive.

Class player creates player objects with score initialized to zero. Each time one player wins we access player.score and increment it by one.

```
 1  # dice game if it is even player 1 point
 2  # odd player 2 gets 1 point
 3  # import random library
 4  import random
 5
 6  # create class player with score intialize to zero
 7  class player:
 8      score = 0
 9
10  # if number is even return True ese return False
11  def is_even(n):
12      even = None
13      if n % 2 == 0:
14          even = True
15      else:
16          even = False
17
18      return even
19
20  # create players
21  player1 = player()
22  player2 = player()
23
24
25  # run loop for 1000 times
26  for i in range(1000):
27      # dice flip , return random number between 1 and 6 inclusive
28      dice = random.randint(1, 6)
29
30      if is_even(dice):
31          player1.score += 1
32      else:
33          player2.score += 1
34
35  print("Player 1 score is: ", player1.score)
36  print("Player 2 score is: ", player2.score)
```

```
Player 1 score is:   518
Player 2 score is:   482
```

We can see that players score are close, which is
expected since each player win probability is 50% as
the ration of odd:even of dice output is 1:1.

Practice Problems

1. Write a program that creates an object of vehicle. The vehicle properties are name, model, color, country of origin and owner.

2. Write a program that simulates a school course. Each course is an object and has variables for name, number of enrolling students, lecturer, hall, department. Create 5 arbitrary courses.

Drawing shapes using pygame

Introduction to pygame

Learning coding is interesting but it's even more interesting and engaging when you're actually making games. While coding a game, you will find yourself applying all the ideas you learnt in this book like loops, conditionals, variables, functions, lists, objects and even more.

For coding games, we will use python library **Pygame**. Pygame is a python library for making games. It was created by Pete Shiners and it enjoys a wide community support.

Installation

To install pygame library on your system follow these steps.

If you are using anaconda <u>Jupyter lab on desktop</u>

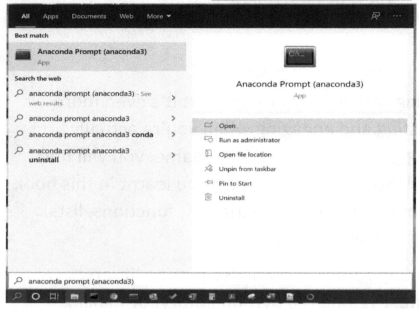

Locate "anaconda Prompt (anaconda3)" on your system.

Click on "anaconda Prompt (anaconda3)" to open it .

In the command prompt type "**pip install pygame**" and press Enter.If installed successful , it should display "**Successfully installed pygame**" massage .

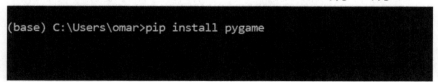

*If you are using the <u>online version of jupyter lab</u> , type "**pip install pygame**" inside the cell and execute the cell*

If you are using <u>notepad++ along with Python</u> , open command prompt

To run your program locate command Prompt on your system and open it.

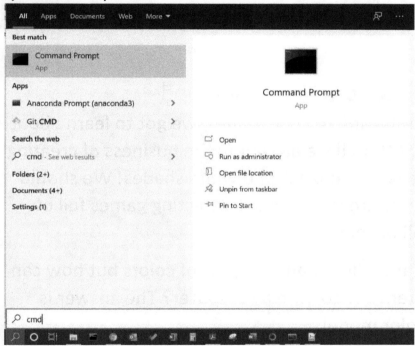

Type **"pip install pygame"** and Enter .

Now you are ready to start coding games !, let's start.

Colors basics – RGB color model

Before starting to code games, we got to learn about colors. After all we are not in the business of creating boring games in black and white shades! We should be able to create colorful interesting games full of life, full of colors.

There are millions and millions of colors but how can we determine color in a computer? The answer is RGB color model.

RGB stands for Red, Green and Blue using 3 corresponding numbers one for each color. We can create any color we want. Each color has a number ranging from 0 to 255 where 0 is null intensity and

255 is the maximum intensity of color. Here are some typical color values

(R, G, B)	Color name
(255, 255, 255)	White
(255, 0, 0)	Red
(0, 255, 0)	Green
(0, 0, 255)	Blue
(0, 0, 0)	Black

To further experiment with RGB, you can find free RGB calculator here

https://www.w3schools.com/colors/colors_rgb.asp

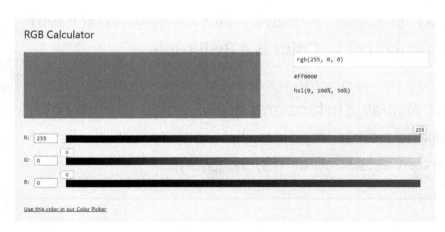

Source: RGB calculator in w3schools

Basic shape creation methods

Let's start learning basic methods to create shapes.

pygame.init() – Initialize pygame and give permissions. This line is essential to start pygame session.

pygame.display.set_mode((X, Y)) – Creates a display window surface with dimension (x,y) where x is width and y is height .This acts as our background.

pygame.display.set_caption('name') – Sets display caption name.

display_surface.fill(color) – Fills display surface with a particular color. Color is a RGB tuple .

pygame.draw.polygon(surface, color, points_list) – Takes display_surface and draws polygon with color color and points in points_list . points_list is a list of cartesian sets such as [(3, 5), (5, 9)].

pygame.draw.line(surface, color, start_point, end_point, thickness) – Draws a line with color col , with starting point start_point and ending point end_point with optional thickness thickness.

pygame.draw.circle(surface, color, center, radius, thickness) -Draws a circle with color color , center center , radius radius and thickness thickness.

pygame.draw.ellipse(surface, color, bounding_rectangle, thickness) – Draws an ellipse bounded and centered by rectangle bounding_rectangle with optional thickness thickness. bounding__rectangle is given by (x, y, width , height) where x and y are upper left corner coordinate, width is rectangle width and height is rectangle height.

pygame.draw.rect(surface, col, (x, y, width, height), thickness) –

Draws a rectangle with color col and coordinates in rectangle_tuple and thickness thickness. (x, y, width, height) is same as bounding_rectangle discussed above.

To read and learn more methods use pygame documentation, Coders read much more than they write. They read others' codes, documentations and manuals. This is a good practice in reading documentation.

https://www.pygame.org/docs/ref/draw.html

pygame coordinate system

pygame default coordinate system origin is centered at upper left (0,0) corner where positive x points rightward and negative y point downward.

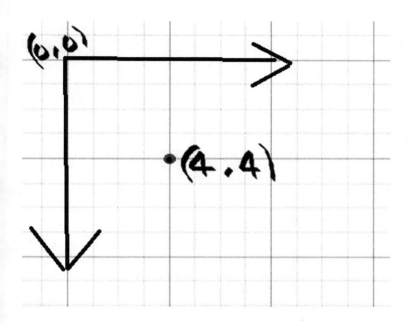

Example 1 Implementing basic drawing methods

In this example we implement the basic pygame drawing methods we discussed in this chapter. We create a circle, ellipse, polygon, square and lines. Each shape is created with its own color, position and size. Try to read and understand this program. It is well commented to facilitate easy reading.

```
1  # import pygame module
2  import pygame
3
4  # activate a pygame library inst .
5  pygame.init()
6
7  # define the RGB value some colors
8  white = (255, 255, 255)
9  black = (0, 0, 0)
10 yellow = (255, 255, 0)
11 red = (255, 0, 0)
12 green = (0, 255, 0)
13 random_color = (120, 30, 50)
14
15
16 # assigning width 600 , height 600 to background
17 dimensions = (600, 600)
18
19 # create the display surface object
20 # of specific dimension..e(X,Y).
21 display = pygame.display.set_mode(dimensions)
22
23 #pygame window name
24 pygame.display.set_caption('Basic shapes')
25
26 # Fill display surface with white
27 # with white colour
28 display.fill(white)
29
30 # draw a polygon using draw.polygon()
31 # pygame.draw.polygon(surface, color,  points_list)
32 pygame.draw.polygon(display, yellow,
33                     [(446, 300), (591, 406),
34                     (536, 577), (356, 577), (300, 406)])
35
36 # draw horizontal line
37 # pygame.draw.line(surface, color, start_point, end_point, thickness)
```

```
38  pygame.draw.line(display, random_color,
39                   (0, 300), (600, 300), 4)
40
41  # draw vertical line
42  pygame.draw.line(display, random_color,
43                   (300, 0), (300, 600), 4)
44
45  # draw a circle
46  # pygame.draw.circle(surface, color, center_point, radius, thickness)
47  pygame.draw.circle(display, red, (150, 150), 50, 0)
48
49  # draw a ellipse pygame.draw.ellipse(surface, color, bounding_rectangle, thickness)
50  pygame.draw.ellipse(display, green, (400, 100, 100, 150), 0)
51
52  # draw a rectangle
53  # pygame.draw.rect(surface, col, (x,y,width,height), thickness)
54  pygame.draw.rect(display, black, (100, 400, 100, 100))
55
56  # infinite loop to keep session on
57  while True :
58
59      # iterate over the list of Event objects
60      # that was returned by pygame.event.get() method.
61      for event in pygame.event.get() :
62
63          # if event object type is QUIT when corner exist button is clicked
64          # then quitting pygame and program
65          if event.type == pygame.QUIT :
66
67              # kill pygame session
68              pygame.quit()
69              # quit the program.
70              quit()
71
72          # Draws the objects screen.
73          pygame.display.update()
```

135

Infinite loop (game loop)

Why do we have infinite loop at line 57? Pygame library is used to create video games. Video is nothing but a continuous stream of pictures viewed in a short amount of time so human eyes can't detect the difference. The loop will keep updating the screen with any newly drawn shapes on it and keeps the session on. Without this infinite loop, Pygame will display the shapes momentarily and cease running. This infinite loop is called the game loop since it is the loop that contains the main logic of a game and is also responsible for updating the screen with any new status.

Output:

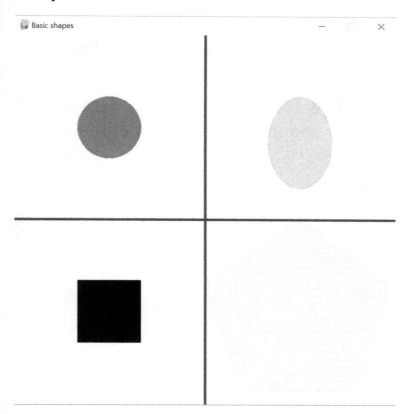

Output is a white background divided into four quadrants. Where a basic shape lives on each quadrant.

Example 2 Frowny face

In this script we create an angry frowny face. This program is very similar to the last example. Except that we draw different shapes. Frowny face basically consists of a 1 circle for face, 2 circles for eyes and an arc for mouth. To understand arc method, read **pygame** documentation. Try to understand how arc gets oriented, you will need it in the practice problems.

```python
2   # import pygame module
3   import pygame
4   import math
5
6   # activate a pygame library inst .
7   pygame.init()
8
9   # define the RGB value some colors
10  white = (255, 255, 255)
11  yellow = (255, 255, 0)
12  red = (255, 0, 0)
13
14  # assigning width 600 , height 600 to background
15  dimensions = (300, 300)
16
17  # create the display surface object
18  display = pygame.display.set_mode(dimensions)
19
20  #pygame window name
21  pygame.display.set_caption("Frowny face !")
22
23  # Display color is white
24  display.fill(white)
25
26  # Draw face
27  pygame.draw.circle(display, yellow, (150, 150), 50, 0)
28
29  # Draw left eye
30  pygame.draw.circle(display, red, (130, 140), 10, 0)
31
32  # Draw right eye
33  pygame.draw.circle(display, red, (170, 140), 10, 0)
34
```

```
32   # Draw right eye
33   pygame.draw.circle(display, red, (170, 140), 10, 0)
34
35   # Draw mouth using arc
36   # arc(surface, color, bounding_rect, start_angle, stop_angle, width=1)
37   pygame.draw.arc(display, red, (135, 175,30,25), 0, math.pi, width=1)
38
39   # infinite loop to keep session on
40   while True :
41       # iterate over the list of Event objects
42       # that was returned by pygame.event.get() method.
43       for event in pygame.event.get() :
44
45           # if event object type is QUIT when corner exist button is clicked
46           # then quitting pygame and program
47           if event.type == pygame.QUIT :
48
49               # kill pygame session
50               pygame.quit()
51               # quit the program.
52               quit()
53
54           # Draws the objects screen.
55           pygame.display.update()
```

Output:

Practice Problems

1. Use frowny face program discussed earlier and turn it into smiley face instead.

2. Create a display of 800 by 800 and create 4 sides connected red boarders and a circle centered at center where it is circumscribed by the boarders.

3. Pick 4 of your favorite emojis and try to draw them using pygame.

4. Create a shape similar to Football pitch picture below.

Animations in Pygame

Animations are images manipulated to appear as moving pictures. To make an animation we create many continues pictures/shapes and view them continuously. The number of times we update the screen is called Frames per second (fps); fps is the number of frames/pictures showed in second. Greater fps numbers make the transitions in videos/games smoother thus increasing the quality. The game loop discussed in earlier chapter is responsible for updating the state of game at fps frame per second. This is how games are made, updating the screen continuously with pictures at a rate human eyes can't distinguish that pictures are in fact discrete.

The figure below shows multiple frames of a running horse. Grouping these frames will result in a running horse video.

The famous horse in motion

Growing square

We make a square that grows in size until it fills the entire lower right screen quadrant. The logic is very similar to how we made various shapes in the previous example except for 2 main differences.

We make pygame clock instance clock=pygame.time.Clock() , this is a pygame method to keep track of time .We use it in the program to control how many frames per seconds (fps) we want using clock.tick(fps). Faster fps updates the shape more frequently which makes the square grows faster.

The second difference is that square side is not fixed anymore. Every loop iteration the square side is increased using line side = 1.01 * side, the screen is cleared (filled with white color) using screen.fill(white) and a new square with the new side size is drawn . Experiment with the value 1.01 , observe how increasing/decreasing this value affect the animation speed .

```python
1   # growing square
2   import pygame
3
4
5   # frames per second to control speed
6   fps = 50
7
8   # Define some colors
9   white = (255, 255, 255)
10  red = (255, 0, 0)
11
12  # A clock instance so we can control frames per second fps
13  clock = pygame.time.Clock()
14
15  # initialize display surface
16  screen = pygame.display.set_mode((500, 500))
17  pygame.display.set_caption("Growing square")
18
19  pygame.init()
20  # white background
21  screen.fill(white)
22
23  # intitial square side legnth
24  side = 50
25
26
27  # game infinite loop
28  loop = True
29  while loop:
30
31      # if quit button press event quit
32      for event in pygame.event.get():
33          if event.type == pygame.QUIT:
34              loop = 0
35
36      pygame.draw.rect(screen, red, (250, 250, side, side))
37      # update frame
38      pygame.display.update()
39
40      # update fps frames per second
41      clock.tick(fps)
42
43      side = 1.01 * side
44      # clear screen
45      screen.fill(white)
46
47
48
49  pygame.quit()
```

146

Output snapshots:

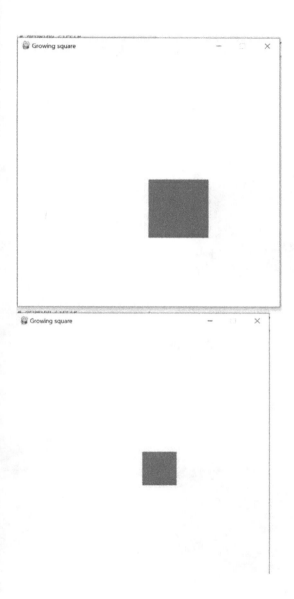

Growing circle

This example is very similar to growing square example. Except that we draw a circle instead of square and increase the radius instead of side length.

```
1   # growing circle
2   import pygame
3
4
5   #  frames per second
6   fps = 50
7
8   # Define some colors
9   white = (255, 255, 255)
10  red = (255, 0, 0)
11
12  # A clock instance so we can control frames per second fps
13  clock = pygame.time.Clock()
14
15  # initialize display surface
16  screen = pygame.display.set_mode((500, 500))
17  pygame.display.set_caption("Growing circle")
18
19  pygame.init()
20  # white background
21  screen.fill(white)
22
23  # game infinite loop
24  loop = True
25
26  # intitial circle radius
27  rad = 50
28
29  while loop:
30
31      # if quit button press event quit
32      for event in pygame.event.get():
33          if event.type == pygame.QUIT:
34              loop = 0
35
36      pygame.draw.circle(screen, red, (250, 250), rad)
```

```
37      # update frame
38      pygame.display.update()

40      # update fps frames per second
41      clock.tick(fps)

43      rad = 1.01 * rad
44      # clear screen
45      screen.fill(white)

47  pygame.quit()
```

Output snapshots:

Moving a ball in different direction

In this example we move a ball in 4 different directions using move_right, move_left, move_up, and move_down functions.

The logic is similar to previous examples, instead of growing shape size every frame we 'grow' object position each time.

The ball starts in the center and keeps moving until it hits border where restarts from center again.

move_right() function works by updating the ball coordinates. The function does not take any inputs because it accesses x and y directly in the global scope because x and y are defined as a global variable.

With each function call the x coordinate is incremented by step size of 2 pixels. The step size determines how smooth the shape moves.

The function makes sure the ball is near border by never incrementing x beyond 480. The background surface size is 500. If x > 480 the ball position is reset to center.

```
28  # global x and y so it have access to outer x and y
29  # right function
30  def move_right():
31      global x,y
32
33      # if ball is near border reset to center
34      if x < 480:
35          x = x + 2
36      else:
37          x = 250
38          y = 250
```

Other function move_left, move_up, and move_down functions are implemented similarly but with changing whether x and y is incremented and detecting a different border.

Read the code below carefully and try to understand it .

```python
1  # moving ball
2  import pygame
3
4
5  #  frames per second
6  fps = 50
7
8  # Define some colors
9  white = (255, 255, 255)
10 red = (255, 0, 0)
11
12 # A clock instance so we can control frames per second fps
13 clock = pygame.time.Clock()
14
15 # initialize display surface
16 screen = pygame.display.set_mode((500, 500))
17 pygame.display.set_caption("moving ball")
18
19 pygame.init()
20 # white background
21 screen.fill(white)
22
23 # initial ball position at center
24 x = 250
25 y = 250
26
27
28 # global x and y so it have access to outer x and y
29 # right function
30 def move_right():
31     global x,y
32
33     # if ball is near border reset to center
34     if x < 480:
35         x = x + 2
36     else:
37         x = 250
38         y = 250
39
```

```
40  # move left
41  def move_left():
42      global x,y
43
44      # if ball is near border reset to center
45      if x > 20:
46          x = x - 2
47      else:
48          x = 250
49          y = 250
50
51  # move up
52  def move_up():
53      global x,y
54
55      # if ball is near border reset to center
56      if y > 20:
57          y = y - 2
58      else:
59          x = 250
60          y = 250
61
62  # move down
63  def move_down():
64      global x,y
65
66      # if ball is near border reset to center
67      if y < 480:
68          y = y + 2
69      else:
70          x = 250
71          y = 250
72
73
74  # game infinite loop
75  loop = True
76
```

```
76
77  while loop:
78
79      # if quit button press event quit
80      for event in pygame.event.get():
81          if event.type == pygame.QUIT:
82              loop = False
83
84      pygame.draw.circle(screen, red, (x, y), 20)
85      # update frame
86      move_right()
87      pygame.display.update()
88      # update fps frames per second
89      clock.tick(fps)
90
91      # clear screen
92      screen.fill(white)
93
94  pygame.quit()
```

Output snapshots:

Moving right

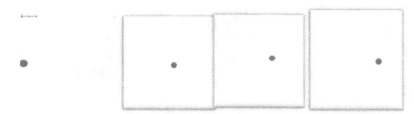

Moving left

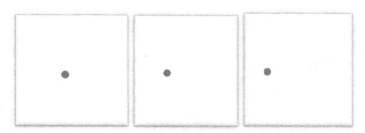

Example 4 Bouncing ball

In this program we create a ball that keep bouncing off borders.

What does it mean for a ball to bounce off border?

Earlier we kept moving the ball by incrementing/decrementing its x and y position by a unit step.

In moving the ball right, we incremented x by 1, while we decremented x by 1 to move it to left. So, to bounce the ball of a given border we need to detect which border it is hitting and increment or decrement the right coordinate x or y.

In bounce function,

stepx = -1 * stepx   , flip x direction if right or left borders touched

stepy = -1 * stepy   , flip y direction if top or bottom borders touched

These lines keep flipping the corresponding coordinate whenever a border is touched.

```python
1   # bouncing ball
2   import pygame
3   import random
4
5
6   #  frames per second
7   fps = 50
8
9   # Define some colors
10  white = (255, 255, 255)
11  red = (255, 0, 0)
12
13  # A clock instance so we can control frames per second fps
14  clock = pygame.time.Clock()
15
16  # initialize display surface
17  screen = pygame.display.set_mode((500, 500))
18  pygame.display.set_caption("bouncing ball")
19
20  pygame.init()
21  # white background
22  screen.fill(white)
23
24  # initial ball position is random
25  x = random.randint(0, 500)
26  y = random.randint(0, 500)
27  stepx = 1
28  stepy = 1
29
30  # global x , y , stepx and stepy so it have access to outer variables
31  # bounce function
32  def bounce():
33      global stepx, stepy, x, y
34
35      # right border and left bounce then make horizontal step negative
36      if x > 480 or x < 20:
37          stepx = -1 * stepx
38
39      # top border and bottom border bounce then make vertical step negative
```

```
31  # bounce function
32  def bounce():
33      global stepx, stepy, x, y
34
35      # right border and left bounce then make horizontal step negative
36      if x > 480 or x < 20:
37          stepx = -1 * stepx
38
39      # top border and bottom border bounce then make vertical step negative
40      if y > 480 or y < 20:
41          stepy = -1 * stepy
42
43      # update x and y
44      x += stepx
45      y += stepy
46
47
48  # game infinite loop
49  loop = True
50
51  while loop:
52
53      # if quit button press event quit
54      for event in pygame.event.get():
55          if event.type == pygame.QUIT:
56              loop = False
57
58      pygame.draw.circle(screen, red, (x, y), 20)
59      # update frame
60      bounce()
61      pygame.display.update()
62      # update fps frames per second
63      clock.tick(fps)
64
65      # clear screen
66      screen.fill(white)
67
68  pygame.quit()
```

Output snapshots:

Bouncing off the top border.

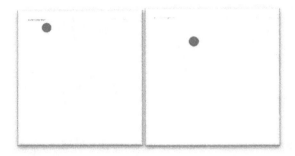

Practice Problems

1. Modify the growing square so it grows form top left corner instead of center.

2. Make a blinking red circle at center that blinks every 2 seconds.

3. Create a shrinking circle, where it starts at radius equal to window size and shrinks to radius 10.

4. Create 2 bouncing balls where they bounce off borders and also bounce of each other if they collide. Hint: in bounce function check for the distance between balls, if close enough trigger a bounce.

Handling Keypress and Mouse Click events

Pygame deal with user inputs mainly using pygame.event module. pygame.event listens and register all events that comes from a keyboard or mouse.Every time event happen an event object is created to record it.

In fact, we have been using pygame.event several times in our programs.

In this snippet, in game loop we continuously check for any new events pygame.event.

pygame.event.get() returns a list of events that occurred since the last pygame.event.get() call.

When the quit button is pressed pygame.event registers this event as event with a type pygame.QUIT .

So we loop through all events and check if any of the events type is pygame.QUIT if so we set loop variable to false to quit the loop in next iteration.

```
27  # game infinite loop
28  loop = True
29  while loop:
30
31      # if quit button press event quit
32      for event in pygame.event.get():
33          if event.type == pygame.QUIT:
34              loop = False
35
```

To read more about pygame events refer to this link :

http://man.hubwiz.com/docset/PyGame.docset/Contents/Resources/Documents/ref/event.html

This table show some of common pygame.event constant and their attributes.

Constant name	Attributes
QUIT	none
ACTIVEEVENT	gain, state
KEYDOWN	, key, mod
KEYUP	key, mod
MOUSEMOTION	pos, rel, buttons
MOUSEBUTTONUP	pos, button
MOUSEBUTTONDOWN	pos, button

Keyboard events

KEYUP and KEYDOWN events have attribute key constants representing keyboard keys.

Using capital k followed by underscore and key name ,

For example F1 is K_F1, w is K_w.

In this snippet, we check when a key is pressed down using pygame.KEYDOWN , we check what arrow key is pressed down and print a message for key name .

```
1  for event in pygame.event.get():
2      if event.type == pygame.QUIT:
3          pygame.quit()
4      elif event.type == pygame.KEYDOWN:
5          if event.key == pygame.K_UP:
6              print("Player moved up!")
7          elif event.key == pygame.K_LEFT:
8              print("Player moved left!")
9          elif event.key == pygame.K_DOWN:
10             print("Player moved down!")
11         elif event.key == pygame.K_RIGHT:
12             print("Player moved right!")
```

To read all key binding, read pygame keys documentation on

https://www.pygame.org/docs/ref/key.html

Mouse events

There are there types of mouse events in pygame .

MOUSEBUTTONDOWN, MOUSEBUTTONUP , and MOUSEMOTION.

MOUSEBUTTONUP , and MOUSEMOTION are received when user presses or moves a mouse.

They have attributes:

Button : 1 for left button , 2 for mouse wheel and 3 for right button .

Pos : Mouse absolute position of mouse (x,y) when button is pressed

MOUSEMOTION is received when user mouse moves, it has 3 attributes

Buttons : tuple of mouse button pressed or not (left, mouse wheel, right)

Pos : absolute cursor position (x,y) in pxels

Rel: position relative to previous position (relative_x, relative_y)

In this example we used to detect mouse using the three discusse mouse attributes .

```
1  # detect mouse actions
2
3  for event in pygame.event.get():
4      if event.type == pygame.QUIT:
5          pygame.quit()
6      elif event.type == pygame.MOUSEMOTION:
7          if event.rel[0] > 0:  # 'rel' is a tuple (x, y). 'rel[0]' is the x-value.
8              print("Moving the mouse to the right")
9          elif event.rel[1] > 0:  # pygame origin is at top left corner so higher y-val mean it further down.
10             print("Moving the mouse down")
11     elif event.type == pygame.MOUSEBUTTONDOWN:
12         if event.button == 1:
13             print("Left mouse button pressed")
14         elif event.button == 3:
15             print("Right mouse button pressed")
16     elif event.type == pygame.MOUSEBUTTONUP:
17         print("Mouse button released")
```

Example 1 : Moving Square

In this example we implement a moving square similar to past chapter but it moves by keyboard keys instead. We detect event of type pygame KEYDOWN then we check for event.

```
1    import pygame
2    import sys
3    pygame.init()
4    fps=30
5    fpsclock=pygame.time.Clock()
6    surface=pygame.display.set_mode((500, 500))
7    pygame.display.set_caption("Moving square")
8    White=(255,255,255)
9    x=10
10   y=10
11   step=5
12   while True:
13       surface.fill(White)
14       pygame.draw.rect(surface, (255,0,0), (x, y, 70, 65))
15       for event in pygame.event.get():
16           if event.type==pygame.QUIT:
17               pygame.quit()
18               sys.exit()
19           elif event.type == pygame.KEYDOWN:
20               if event.key == pygame.K_LEFT:
21                   x -= step
22               elif event.key == pygame.K_UP:
23                   y -= step
24               elif event.key == pygame.K_RIGHT:
25                   x += step
26               elif event.key == pygame.K_DOWN:
27                   y += step
28
29       pygame.display.update()
30       fpsclock.tick(fps)
```

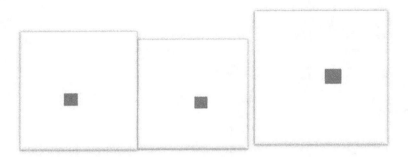

Example : Moving Square by Mouse .

In this example we let the square follow the mouse by updating the square position with the mouse cursor position.We access mouse cursor position pygame. MOUSEMOTION , mouse x position is event.pos[0] and y position is event.pos[y].We also change the color of square if mouse left button is clicked using pygame.MOUSEBUTTONUP.

```
1   import pygame
2   import sys
3   pygame.init()
4   fps=30
5   fpsclock=pygame.time.Clock()
6   surface=pygame.display.set_mode((500, 500))
7   pygame.display.set_caption("Moving square by mouse")
8   White=(255,255,255)
9   Black = (0, 0, 0)
10  red = (255, 0, 0)
11  x=10
12  y=10
13  step=5
14  color = red
15  while True:
16      surface.fill(White)
17      pygame.draw.rect(surface, color, (x, y, 70, 65))
18      for event in pygame.event.get():
19          if event.type==pygame.QUIT:
20              pygame.quit()
21              sys.exit()
22          elif event.type == pygame.MOUSEMOTION:          # detect mouse motion
23              # assign x,y to cursor positon
24              x,y = event.pos[0], event.pos[1]            # move square to mouse location
25          elif event.type == pygame.MOUSEBUTTONDOWN:
26              if event.button == 1:                       # while left clicked square color is black else red
27                  color = Black
28          elif event.type == pygame.MOUSEBUTTONUP:
29              if event.button == 1:
30                  color = red
31
32
33      pygame.display.update()
34      fpsclock.tick(fps)
35
36
```

Practice Problems

1. Write a program of moving ball by following mouse cursor. When left mouse button is clicked the ball keeps growing. When right mouse button is clicked the ball shrinks.

2. Make hidden treasure seeker game, where once the mouse clicks at a specific hidden 10x10 square it change color to red and prints treasure found.

3. Make a signaling traffic light.

4. Implement a ball that bounces when space bar is clicked.

Pong game

This game builds on "Bouncing Ball" game discussed earlier. The game consists of a paddle moving horizontally on floor and a bouncing ball bouncing of the game window borders. Player moves the paddle so to bounce the ball up never letting it touch the 'ground'. Player moves the paddle by pointing the mouse to intended direction.

In the game loop, infinite loop, ball is moves using move_ball() function which updates the ball position .Then , we draw the ball at its new location and move the paddle to where the mouse pointer points. We update display at fps frame per second. Fps is set at 80 frame per second. We can make the game more challenging/faster by increasing this number.
It is always a good idea to read any game code in a top down approach, starting first at the main game loop getting high level idea about how the game operates. Then delving into functions definitions and understanding them one by on. The snippet below is our game loop.

Now that you have a high-level idea about the game you can read the complete program. The code is well commented for the ease of reading.

```python
1  # pong game
2  import pygame
3  from random import choice
4
5  # Game frames per second to control game speed
6  fps = 80
7
8  # Define some colors
9  white = (255, 255, 255)
10 black = (0, 0, 0)
11 red = (255, 0, 0)
12 green = (0, 255, 0)
13
14 # initial ball coordinates
15 x_ball = 500
16 y_ball = 300
17
18 # direction to capture where the ball is heading
19 horizontal_direction = 'left'
20 vertical_direction = 'down'
21
22 # Eachtime ball is server, score is incremented
23 score = 0
24
25 # The step where ball postion is updated
26 step = 2
27
28 # A clock instance so we can control frames per second fps
29 clock = pygame.time.Clock()
30
31 # initialize display surface
32 screen = pygame.display.set_mode((500, 500))
33 pygame.display.set_caption("Pong game")
34
35 pygame.init()
36
```

```
37
38  # Draw the ball at x_ball, y_ball
39  def ball():
40      pygame.draw.circle(screen, red, (x_ball, y_ball), 10, 10)
41
42  # draw paddle at x, y
43  def paddle(x,y):
44      pygame.draw.rect(screen, black, (x, y, 80, 10))
45
46  # move ball by a step
47  def move_ball():
48      global x_ball, y_ball, horizontal_direction, vertical_direction
49      # if ball is going to left decrement x_ball so it continues left
50      if horizontal_direction == "left":
51          x_ball -= step
52
53          # if ball is near left border reflect to right
54          if x_ball < 10:
55              horizontal_direction = "right"
56
57      # if ball is going downward increment y_ball so it continues downward
58      if vertical_direction == 'down':
59          y_ball += step
60
61      # if ball is going upward decrement y_ball so it continues upward
62      if vertical_direction == 'up':
63          y_ball -= step
64
65          # if ball is near upper border reflect downward
66          if y_ball < 10:
67              vertical_direction = 'down'
68
69      # if ball is going right increment x_ball so it continues right
70      if horizontal_direction == "right":
71          x_ball += step
72
```

```
73          # if ball is near right border reflect left
74          if x_ball > 480:
75              horizontal_direction = "left"
76
77
78  # function to detect serving the ball by paddle
79  def served():
80      global x_ball, y_ball # ball x and y
81      global x, y            # paddle x, y
82      global horizontal_direction, vertical_direction, step
83      global score
84
85      # detect if ball is heading to paddle
86      if horizontal_direction == "left":
87          if y_ball > 480:
88
89              # ball is touching the paddle
90              if x_ball >= x and  x_ball < x + 50:
91                  print("Good job")
92                  # increment score
93                  score += 1
94                  # flip direction
95                  vertical_direction = "up"
96                  step = 1
97
98              # if ball missed reset ball coordinates and decrement score
99              else:
100                 pygame.draw.circle(screen, black, (x_ball, y_ball), 10, 10)
101                 pygame.display.update()
102                 x_ball, y_ball = 500, 300
103                 score -= 1
104
105         # print score in caption
106         pygame.display.set_caption(f"Your score is: {score}")
107
```

```
111  while loop:
112      # detect pressed keys
113      keys = pygame.key.get_pressed()
114
115      # if quit button press event quit
116      for event in pygame.event.get():
117          if event.type == pygame.QUIT:
118              loop = 0
119      # get mouse pointer coordinates
120      x, y = pygame.mouse.get_pos()
121
122      # move the ball by a step
123      move_ball()
124      # draw ball
125      ball()
126      # draw paddle at mouse x coordinate
127      paddle(x,490)
128      # is the ball served
129      served()
130      # update frame
131      pygame.display.update()
132      # white background
133      screen.fill(white)
134      # update fps frames per second
135      clock.tick(fps)
136
137
138
139  pygame.quit()
```

Output:

Your score is: 1

Practice Problems

1. After playing with pong game. You probably observed that when balls reset position, it always starts from the same position. Make a function that resets the ball at different random position each time it reset.

2.In Pong game, edit the code so you can use keyboard arrows to move the paddle.

3.In Pong game, implement a second player with a paddle on the top border. Each player must have his own score.

Conclusion

Congrats on getting through to the end of this book. You are definitely on the right track.

If you'd like a more beginner friendly version of this book, you can download my Coding for Kids and Beginners using Python.

If you're more interested in JavaScript, you can download my Coding for Kids Ages 9-15 and Coding for Kids Ages 10 and Up

Other Recommended Books for further reading:

Python Crash Course

Automate the Boring Stuff with Python

Learn Python Quickly

CPSIA information can be obtained
at www.ICGtesting.com
Printed in the USA
BVHW052033261222
654951BV00015B/617

9 781922 462534